Raising Test Scores

for ALL STUDENTS

Raising Test Scores

for ALL STUDENTS

An Administrator's Guide to Improving Standardized Test Performance

Eugene Kennedy

CORWIN PRESS, INC.
A Sage Publications Company
Thousand Oaks, California

For information:

Corwin Press, Inc.
A Sage Publications Company
2455 Teller Road
Thousand Oaks, California 91320
www.corwinpress.com

Sage Publications Ltd.
6 Bonhill Street
London EC2A 4PU
United Kingdom

Sage Publications India Pvt. Ltd.
B-42, Panchsheel Enclave
Post Box 4109
New Delhi 110 017 India

Printed in the United States of America

Library of Congress Cataloging-in-Publication Data

Kennedy, Eugene, Ph. D.
Raising test scores for all students: An administrator's guide
to standardized test performance / Eugene Kennedy.
      p. cm.
ISBN 0-7619-4527-X (cloth) — ISBN 0-7619-4528-8 (paper)
   1. Educational tests and measurements-United States. 2. Education-Aims
and objectives-United States. 3. School improvement programs-United
States. I. Title: Administrator's guide to standardized test performance.
II. Title.
LB3051 .K34 2003
371.26'2—dc211
                                        2002153689

03   04   05   06   10   9   8   7   6   5   4   3   2   1

Acquisitions Editor:	Rachel Livsey
Editorial Assistant:	Phyllis Cappello
Production Editor:	Melanie Birdsall
Copy Editor:	Toni Williams
Typesetter:	C&M Digitals (P) Ltd.
Indexer:	Kathy Paparchontis
Proofreader:	Teresa Herlinger
Cover Designer:	Michael Dubowe
Production Artist:	Lisa Miller

Contents

Preface

Standardized Testing in Schools

Standardized tests are so ubiquitous in today's schools, it must seem to many that they have always been around. In fact, their often intrusive presence is a fairly recent event. Imagine that not long ago there were no test drills, no gut-wrenching questions about lost booklets, no faculty terrified that student performance on "the test" would not meet state or district standards. Today, however, some form of high-stakes standardized testing exists in almost every public school in the United States. Moreover, it is not an exaggeration to say that in many of these schools, conventional educational processes are frequently suspended in deference to test preparation activities. Furthermore, the stakes are so high and the pressure to perform so intense that students, teachers, and administrators are often pushed to the psychological and ethical breaking point.

Almost all would agree that the pressure generated by standardized tests is often counterproductive. Nevertheless, the reality of modern schooling in this country is that these tests are widely used to make significant educational decisions. For example, in most accountability programs, whether the focus is on students, teachers, or an entire school or district, the performance of students on standardized tests is a key component. For students, these tests may determine if they will be promoted from one grade to another or if they will receive their high school diplomas. For teachers, the pressures are equally great: Students' outcomes on standardized tests are often directly linked to annual evaluations and merit pay raises, may impact the relationship a teacher has with his or her colleagues and administrators, and can lead to reassignment, transfer, or even unemployment. For administrators, these tests are events which largely determine the reputation of their schools. They can be the basis for public rewards or the justification for demoralizing sanctions.

Why This Book

Criticisms of standardized testing in schools have been vociferous, frequent, and, in some instances, effective. However, President George W. Bush's No Child Left Behind (NCLB) legislation represents a major shift by the federal government toward those who favor a more, not less, prominent role for standardized tests in schools. In the wake of this legislation, the question is not *if* there will be standardized testing in schools, but rather, *how much?* Given the financial backing of the federal government and the explicit calls in the legislation for annual assessments and increased test-based accountability, this law has the potential to expand testing as never before. It is quite likely, a decade from now, that school accreditation and funding, teacher certification and employment, and perhaps the licensure of school administrators will have an unprecedented dependency on student outcomes on standardized tests.

With the stakes associated with standardized tests being as high as they are, it behooves school administrators to take the steps necessary to ensure that their students will perform as well as possible. The danger, and there is plenty of evidence to support this, is that efforts to prepare students for high-stakes tests may lessen the quality of teaching and learning occurring in schools (e.g., see Haladyna, Nolen, & Haas, 1991; Johnson & Johnson, 2002; Mehrens & Kaminski, 1989). This book describes and illustrates a model for preparing students to do well on standardized tests while not disrupting the normal teaching and learning process. This book is *not* a collection of recipes and strategies for defeating test items or misleading graders of exams or performances. Instead, I describe a series of steps which guide school administrators through the process of isolating and addressing problems which interfere with student performance on the types of standardized achievement tests which are the backbone of most state and local accountability programs. The model described in this book is based on common features of widely recognized school improvement programs (Effective Schools, Accelerated Schools, the Little Red Schoolhouse, etc.) and although components of the model may sound familiar, I hope the reader will find their explicit application to the issue of test preparation of practical use. The presentation is brief and concise—I expect that anyone thumbing through the pages of this text is looking for ideas and answers to practical problems, not a protracted discussion of historical or theoretical import. The material and samples are based on experience and reflect those practices I have found to be most useful.

Audience and Purpose

This book was written for school administrators and leaders. It should be used to either evaluate the process a school uses to prepare students for standardized tests or to design a comprehensive strategy. It is likely that most principals and other school leaders will recognize some features (good or bad) of their current test preparation process in this book. It is my hope that they will find ideas discussed in this text that they have not yet considered or addressed.

Organization of the Book

There are eight chapters in this book. Chapter 1, "A Review of the Nature of Standardized Tests," presents a foundation and overview of standardized tests. The assumption of this chapter is that the reader may have some prior knowledge of the subject but may not be well versed on these topics. I present a brief history of the standardized testing movement in this country and turn to a discussion of the nature and variety of standardized measures most frequently used in education. I end the chapter with a review of the ways in which standardized tests can be used to aid the educational enterprise and a discussion of the competencies school administrators and teachers need to effectively make use of their potential. Several technical terms (e.g., reliability) are introduced in this chapter.

Chapter 2, "Standardized Test Preparation for Schools: A Model," presents the school test preparation model that is at the heart of the book. It begins with a discussion of organizational change and the need for administrators to adopt a schoolwide approach to improvement and change. Next, several school improvement and change movements in education are discussed. These include Accelerated Schools and Effective Schools, among others. The common features of these models are highlighted and the process of adapting these principles to test preparation is then discussed. Finally, the basic four-step model is briefly described. The remaining chapters of the book are devoted to explaining and illustrating the steps of this model.

Chapter 3, "Adopting a Systemic Approach to Improvement and Change," describes the steps administrators can take to effect a systemic change in the way their school prepares students for standardized tests. For each of the steps described, specific guidelines are developed and examples provided.

Chapter 4, "Aligning the Educational Process With Desired Outcomes," describes the process of understanding the target for change: the standardized test. The process includes several steps, which start with gathering information on the structure and content of the target examination and end with procedures for identifying and prioritizing problem areas.

Chapter 5, "Aligning the Educational Process With Inputs," describes the steps the reader can follow to ensure that the test preparation process of the school aligns with the characteristics of the students, faculty, staff, and community in which the school is located. Various techniques for gathering and analyzing relevant data are described.

Chapter 6, "Creating Positive Change," focuses on synthesis of the information gathered in previous steps. The intent is to identify and connect problems noted in previous steps. From this, goals, objectives, and benchmarks are set. Procedures for accomplishing this are discussed and examples provided. The chapter also includes a discussion of strategies for implementing and monitoring the intervention.

Chapter 7, "A Case Study of an Elementary School," written by Dr. Leslie F. Jones-Hamilton, describes a case study of an elementary school in which the model was adopted and applied. Although the name and location of the school are fictitious, the data reflect realistic patterns. The purpose of this chapter is to give the reader a step-by-step example of how the model developed in this text can be employed.

Chapter 8, "Conclusion," reemphasizes the central idea that this is a systemic change model which involves a long-term commitment. The philosophy and logic of the model are reiterated and suggestions for next steps are offered to the reader.

ACKNOWLEDGMENTS

This book is the product of many years of workshops, presentations, and a variety of other activities all focused on one objective: improving the performance of students on standardized tests. Over the years I have learned a great deal from educators concerned about student outcomes on standardized tests. Many of the ideas I had about test preparation two decades ago have changed dramatically. This book reflects what I learned from sincere and honest educators who struggle valiantly to help students succeed. I owe a great debt of gratitude to them, one and all. I also wish to thank the reviewers of an earlier draft of this manuscript. Their encouraging, thoughtful, and detailed comments have made this a much better text than it might otherwise have been.

The contributions of the following reviewers are gratefully acknowledged:

Linda L. Elman
Director of Research and Evaluation
Central Kitsap School District
Silverdale, WA

Mike Harmon
Program Manager, Test Administration
Georgia Department of Education
Atlanta, GA

Diane R. Garavaglia
Senior Research Analyst
American Institutes for Research
Washington, D.C.

Nancy Law
Educational Consultant
Former Director of Research
Sacramento City Schools
Sacramento, CA

Roberta Glaser
Assistant Superintendent
St. Johns Public Schools
St. Johns, MI

Rose H. Weiss
Adjunct Professor of Education
Nova Southeastern University
Fort Lauderdale, FL

Catherine Thome
Academic Coordinator
Lake County Educational Services
Grayslake, IL

References

Haladyna, T. M., Nolen, S. B., & Haas, N. S. (1991). Raising standardized achievement test scores and the origins of test score pollution. *Educational Researcher, 20,* 2-7.

Johnson, D., & Johnson, B. (2002). *High stakes: Children, testing and failure in American schools.* Lanham, MD: Rowman and Little.

Mehrens, W. A., & Kaminski, J. (1989). Methods of improving standardized test scores: Fruitful, fruitless, or fraudulent? *Educational Measurement: Issues and Practices, 8,* 14-22.

About the Author

Eugene Kennedy is an Associate Professor of Educational Research Methodology at Louisiana State University in Baton Rouge, Louisiana. He is the Interim Chair for the Department of Educational Leadership, Research and Counseling. He teaches courses in educational measurement, statistics, and research. His current research interests include school effectiveness and accountability. He has published numerous articles and written several chapters in books. He has been a national consultant on test preparation for more than two decades.

1

A Review
of the
Nature of
Standardized
Tests

This chapter presents an overview of standardized tests and their applications in education. The first section presents a brief historical review of standardized testing in schools. This is followed by a discussion of the nature of these tests and their uses in education. Several technical terms (e.g., reliability) are introduced and discussed.

A Brief History of
Standardized Testing in America

Large-scale standardized testing in the United States can be traced to the First World War. At the beginning of U.S. involvement in the war, the military was overwhelmed with volunteers. At the time, much of the country, including the military, was deeply immersed in the efficiency movement. The idea, borrowed from the industrial workplace, was to use input, including human capital, in such a manner as to maximize output and minimize waste. Subscribing to this idea, the U.S. military was committed to finding scientific ways to maximize the efficiency with which it used human capital for its war machine. A solution was offered by leaders of the American Psychological Association (APA).

Headed by Robert Yerkes, the APA proposed developing an objective and scientific way for planners to allocate men to positions in the military hierarchy. Yerkes and his colleagues proposed and developed two tests designed to measure the mental ages of recruits and volunteers. The Army Alpha test was developed for examinees who could read and the Army Beta test was developed for those who could not. These examinations were administered to nearly two million young men. The military used the test results to classify examinees for various posts, ranging from those selected for officer training to those who were labeled "morons" or "imbeciles" and dismissed.

The results of the Army testing project were widely considered to have been a phenomenal success. In fact, within a few decades after the war, the number and variety of standardized tests had increased exponentially and there was almost no sector of U.S. society untouched by the standardized testing movement (e.g., see Haney, 1984). As Popham (2000) noted, "Almost anyone who could crank out multiple-choice items and bundle them together, or so it appeared, began publishing group aptitude or achievement tests" (p. 19). As some observers have noted, were it not for the success of the military testing project, it is possible that the standardized testing movement in this country would have remained largely an academic pursuit and not have taken center stage in educational policies and reforms (see Haney, 1984).

The Growth of Educational Testing

Shortly after World War I, the Scholastic Aptitude Test (SAT) was developed and adopted by many colleges for admissions purposes. Achievement tests developed by E. L. Thorndike at Columbia University began to find their way into schools and districts across the country. Driven by legislation which mandated schooling of immigrants, standardized tests played an increasing role in the educational process. Standardized intelligence and achievement tests were seen by proponents as tools which could bring efficiency to schooling by (a) providing a means of allocating a diverse population of students to educational experiences which were best suited to their "native" abilities, and (b) providing policymakers and the public with an objective and fair assessment of actual achievement (see Cronbach, 1975).

The rate of growth of standardized testing increased with the arrival of high-speed computing. Computers made it possible to score multiple-choice exams electronically and in a fraction of the time required to score them by hand. The result was to make testing of millions both practical and economically feasible. As a result, large-scale standardized testing grew rapidly and by the middle of the 20th century almost all school systems were involved in some form. The federal government gave momentum to this movement in the 1960s by requiring that standardized achievement tests be used to gauge the success of the massive Title I programs funded under the Elementary and Secondary Education Act of 1965 (ESEA; see Brooks & Pakes, 1993).

Accompanying the growth of standardized testing was a new professional, the psychometrician or measurement specialist. These individuals were trained in the traditions of quantitative psychologists and statisticians. The specialists provided the technical foundations for the testing movement. Their jargon and technical sophistication made their discipline virtually inaccessible to most educational practitioners. Backed by large testing companies and corporations, testing specialists defined standards for the development and use of educational and psychological assessments so much so that in time assessments for high-stakes educational decisions were seen to be beyond the ability of educational practitioners (see Haney, 1984).

Trends and Challenges
In Standardized Testing

The testing boom which began in the 1920s on the heels of the Army Alpha and Beta project drew criticism and controversy, but nothing like what occurred in the 1960s. With the growth of psychometrics as a distinct discipline and the tendency of political leaders to turn to standardized testing as a policy tool, the number of tests administered in schools increased and the types of decisions based on test scores also increased. By the late 1960s, most states had extensive standardized testing programs. These programs linked test results to such a growing variety of high-stakes decisions that even proponents of standardized testing often questioned some of their uses (see Haney, 1984). The inevitable result was backlash. The 1960s saw a variety of widely read and influential criticisms of standardized testing, perhaps culminating in the call by several influential educational organizations for a moratorium on all standardized testing in schools (e.g., see Bandesh, 1962; Gould, 1981).

The criticisms of the 1960s focused on many aspects of testing programs, but a key problem was the relevance of standardized testing for classroom decisions. Attracted by the air of scientific objectivity, policymakers often ignored the fact that most standardized tests only partially matched local curriculum and provided little information about the skills and abilities students actually had. The results of these criticisms and general social concerns about the quality of education provided to children led to the criterion-referenced and minimum competency testing movements (see Mehrens & Lehmann, 1991). Unlike traditional standardized tests, these new tests were designed to provide information about what students could and could not do, and to certify whether students had met minimum performance standards.

If the criterion-referenced testing (CRT) and minimum competency testing movements changed the nature of standardized tests and promoted mandatory testing, *A Nation at*

Risk and related publications raised the stakes to a level not seen before (National Commission on Excellence in Education, 1983). The famous conclusion of this report, which pointed to poorly performing schools as a threat to national security, resonated with the public and policymakers in the early 1980s and served to place state mandated high-stakes testing at the front of the educational agenda. Not long after this report was released, mandated standardized testing existed in nearly every state. These tests were linked to student promotions, teacher evaluations, school evaluations, and so on. The pressure, however, of high-stakes testing and accountability often led to questionable educational practices. While the normal expectation was that these problems primarily involved teacher activities such as providing inappropriate aid for students, an article published in the late 1980s posed the prospect that even large testing companies were somehow responsible for polluting the quality of the educational process. A West Virginia physician reported that while he treated children who could barely read, he was astounded to find that they had high scores on standardized reading tests (Cannell, 1988). More important, he observed that nearly all states reported the impossible results that they were above the national average. The resulting question was whether testing companies were in collusion with state departments of education. These criticisms served to draw attention to test use, test preparation practices, and, most important, the impact of testing on teaching and learning (see Haladyna, 2002).

Questions about how tests scores affected the teaching and learning process in schools reached a crescendo in the mid-1990s and led to what has been termed the authentic testing movement. The multiple-choice item, which had been the hallmark of standardized tests since the Army Alpha and Beta tests, was seen to be limited in the types of skills it assessed and was believed to promote and reflect a behaviorist/mastery perspective on learning (Shepard, 1991). In the 1990s, much of the educational community had begun to feel that learning and thinking were more complicated than the simple mastery learning, input–output model implied by the multiple-choice item. Perhaps best captured in a classic paper by Grant Wiggins was the call for a new form of test, one in which students are encouraged to think, for which there may not be just one right answer (Wiggins, 1989). The impact of this movement was to once again change the nature of standardized tests. Traditional multiple-choice items were, if not completely replaced, given a far less prominent role in testing programs, replaced by open-ended items, performances, and other tasks thought to be more consistent with the complexity of the ways in which children think and learn.

The current trend in standardized testing is toward what has been referred to as the standards movement. The idea is that not only should tests be more consistent with the ways in which people think and learn, but the content of the test and the criterion for performance should both reflect the highest standards with respect to national and international goals and norms. It should be noted that there is considerable debate on the quality and usefulness of state standards and their appropriate role in education (Falk, 2000).

No Child Left Behind

The Elementary and Secondary Education Act of 1965 was designed to redress discrepancies in educational outcomes among students, which seemed to be linked to differences in socioeconomic background. The Title I provision of the act provided funds for schools serving large percentages of low-income students, but added the caveat that schools needed to demonstrate their effectiveness using standardized tests. The impact was a dramatic increase in the use of standardized testing in schools. The current reauthorization of ESEA, known as No Child Left Behind (NCLB), promises to expand high-stakes testing as never before (for more information, see www.ed.gov/legislation/ESEA02/). NCLB redirects federal support for education to local school systems and specifically calls for the following:

- Mandatory testing of all students in Grades 3 through 8
- Use of test results to evaluate the performance of schools
- Reporting of test results to parents and other stakeholders

More than previous versions of this law, standardized tests are at the heart of NCLB. This bill also explicitly links students' outcomes on standardized tests with significant consequences for schools and educators. These consequences include recognition and rewards for schools that meet growth targets and interventions and the prospect of closure for those that do not.

What Do School Administrators Need to Know About Standardized Tests?

Because of the obvious growth of standardized testing and the increase in consequences of student outcomes on these tests, it is important for school administrators to be well versed in the use of standardized tests and knowledgeable of their basic character. The following section presents information on the basic structure of standardized tests.

BASIC CHARACTERISTICS OF A STANDARDIZED TEST

Standardized Testing

What Is a Standardized Test?

The most direct answer to this question is that a standardized test is an examination administered under strictly uniform conditions and interpreted in a consistent manner. The essence of this definition is that all the key aspects of testing are uniform. The same test is administered to all examinees, the conditions under which the test is administered are standardized (time, resources, etc.), and the ways in which scores are interpreted are likewise standardized.

What Is the Advantage or Motivation for Standardization?

To answer this question, it is insightful to once again consider history. While some form of testing has been around as long as schools have existed, for most of that history tests were either oral or essay-based. Examinees were given questions by an instructor or committee and responses were evaluated. The questions were not necessarily of the same difficulty and responses were not necessarily given the same degree of scrutiny. Allegations of cheating, favoritism, and a host of other problems led to many challenges and disputes. These issues reached something of a crisis when widely reported research studies demonstrated that the grades teachers assigned to essays and math exams varied dramatically from one teacher to another and from one occasion to another for the same teacher (see Haney, 1984).

Modern ideas about testing developed from the work of experimental psychologists interested in measuring human capacities which could not be easily quantified. These included intelligence, hearing, and sensory acuity. A guiding principle of this movement was the concept of experimental control, which proposed that measurements of human subjects should be made under strict laboratory conditions. This meant that scientists and their assistants would make their observations and measurements under specified environmental conditions, in a specified way, and adhere to professional guidelines in interpreting their results—the goal being to gain a precise and accurate measurement of the subject. These principles were transferred from the laboratory and adapted to the measurement of attributes such as intelligence, achievement, and beliefs, as well as a host of others. It is this adaptation that gives the standardized tests we encounter in schools their distinct characteristics. Whether the focus is on intelligence, achievement, attitudes, or some other attribute, calling a measure a standardized assessment implies that (a) it has been carefully constructed to measure the construct of interest, (b) the conditions under which the examination should be administered are specified and carefully controlled, (c) the way in which responses are scored is specified, and (d) the way in which scores are interpreted, that is, their meaning, follows precise rules. It is hoped that these tools will lead to accurate measurements. In the next sections we focus more specifically on the construction of standardized tests.

The Construction of Standardized Tests

It can be said that one of the best strategies for confronting a challenge is a good understanding of its nature. With that in mind, we focus on the development and construction of standardized tests. Although there are many different types of standardized measures, as discussed below, for the moment we focus on measures of academic achievement. Typically, constructing a standardized achievement test involves the following tasks: (a) specifying the construct the test is intended to measure, (b) developing items or tasks to measure the desired constructs, and (c) administering the test and analyzing results for evidence of its quality and for purposes of constructing interpretive aids.

Specifying the Construct

In a typical classroom, a teacher might identify the objectives covered over the past three weeks. The teacher might then determine the importance of each objective and develop a corresponding number of related items. The process is similar with respect to the construction of a standardized measure; however, the scope is different. Because a standardized test is a major undertaking, test companies strive to develop measures that are as widely applicable as possible. With regard to achievement, to increase the relevance of their test, developers select a specific content area and grade level and devise a test which measures those things that are commonly taught or expected of students across the country. This might mean obtaining copies of curriculum guides from hundreds of school districts and dozens of state education agencies. Widely used textbooks, instructional materials, and guidelines published by professional associations might also be collected for purposes of review. These documents would all be carefully screened and analyzed by measurement experts, content experts, and practitioners in an effort to identify the most commonly addressed instructional outcomes. These outcomes would form the content domain of the test. It is important to note that this domain is an abstraction and might not actually exist in any school district or any school in the population for which the test was designed. It therefore becomes important for prospective users of a test to correlate their local instructional objectives with the content domain represented in the test.

The development process applies to tests targeted for a national audience. However, the same issues exist for tests tailored for specific states or even school districts. Since the early 1970s, most states have developed statewide assessment programs which include a standardized test developed specifically to reflect students' mastery of the state's curriculum. In the past, these were largely criterion-referenced tests designed to reflect whether students had met minimum performance levels. More recently, state curriculum frameworks specify not only content standards (what students ought to know), but also performance standards (what students ought to be able to do). Standards-based assessments tend to report performance in terms of the proficiency levels of students, with many states making use of some variant of the reporting scheme for the National Assessment of Educational Progress (NAEP): Advanced, Proficient, Basic, and Unsatisfactory (see the NAEP Web site at http://nces.ed.gov/nationsreportcard/).

The controversy associated with standards-based state assessment programs stems from the fact that the implementation of the state curriculum can vary dramatically from one setting to another. These variations have to do with the competencies of teachers, especially their ability to implement classroom innovations; the resource differentials which exist between and within school systems; and the external supports which may vary dramatically from one community to another. The impact of these factors is such that the printed curriculum and the taught curriculum may differ, and these differences may not be simply due to random chance. It is therefore important for school-based personnel to exercise caution in drawing inferences from student performances on national or state standardized tests.

Items and Tasks

Turning again to our discussion of the development of standardized tests, once the content domain and emphasis of the test have been defined, the next step is to construct or select the test items. A typical classroom teacher might simply choose items from the instructor's manual which accompanied the text or she might develop her own. In either event, if the items appeared to pose problems for students, they might be discarded and not used in future tests. Contrast this with the item development process of a large testing company. First, there is likely to be an entire staff of professional item writers. These are typically content experts that have been trained in matching item formats to instructional objectives and in writing items that avoid many of the pitfalls (e.g., ambiguity) of the typical classroom tests. The items are drafted, undergo an extensive internal review for technical quality and content appropriateness, are likely to be reviewed by a bias review committee, and will then undergo extensive field tests in the target population. The field-test results contain information on the item's difficulty, discrimination, and a host of other characteristics. As typically used, item difficulty refers to the percentage of respondents who respond correctly to an item, and discrimination is a measure of an item's ability to distinguish between more and less knowledgeable examinees. These statistics, as well as others, determine if an item will be included in an actual test.

Technical Characteristics of Standardized Tests

Once the items have met whatever criteria are set, the test is assembled and the question of the quality of the test is raised. The question of quality among measurement specialists is usually answered by examining the reliability and validity of the measure.

Reliability

In popular use, reliability refers to the extent to which one obtains consistent results with some thing or process. For example, a reliable automobile is one that consistently starts when the ignition is turned, a reliable employee consistently shows up for work when scheduled, and a reliable performer consistently yields good (or bad) performances. The point is that the question of quality, for most people, is intricately linked to the notion of consistency. Few people, for instance, would be satisfied with an automobile that could only be expected to start 50% of the time. Similarly, when it comes to measurements of human attributes, a quality measure should yield consistent scores when an individual's standing on the attribute has not changed. For example, if I were to stand on a scale and record my weight, step off the scale, and a moment later repeat the process, by all accounts, the numbers I record should be the same. If they are not, then there is something problematic about this measurement procedure. Perhaps I was not particularly careful in recording the measurements, or perhaps the scale suffers from some mechanical malady which leads it to yield varying weights for a given object. In either event, the lack of consistency in results is clearly a problem, one which would threaten my confidence in the quality of the resulting scores and the usefulness of the procedure.

In the context of educational achievement, the notion of consistency is still intricately linked to assessments of the quality of an examination. In fact, estimates of the reliability of a test can be thought of as indexes of the extent to which the test yields consistent scores for examinees. There are many different ways of estimating the reliability of a test. These techniques differ largely with respect to the types of inconsistency they detect.

Test–Retest Estimates of Reliability. The test–retest technique for estimating reliability entails administering the same test to a group of examinees on two distinct occasions. Of course, this is only reasonable if the attribute measured by the exam is expected to be stable over time. As such, these indexes are typically only reported for measures of intelligence, aptitude, and other characteristics expected to remain stable or change very slowly. If the scores of examinees are not similar on the two occasions, then the inference is that scores on the exam are subject to random errors.

Reliability Estimates Based on Equivalent Forms. It is not uncommon for test developers to have multiple forms of the same test. This is necessary for purposes of makeup exams, educational research using a pre–post design, and so on. Because the two forms of the exam will not consist of the same items, administering both forms to the same examinees provides valuable information. One interpretation is that the scores should be the same unless the responses of examinees are affected by extraneous factors.

Internal Consistency Estimates of Reliability. Among the most commonly reported forms of reliability are measures of internal consistency. These indexes reflect the extent to which the items in a test yield consistent outcomes for examinees. If the items measure dramatically different constructs, this type of evidence could be misleading. However, most tests have multiple items designed to measure the same or very similar skills. Comparing examinee performance across the items yields valuable information about consistency. Some of the more popular measures of internal consistency are the split-half estimates, Kuder–Richardson formulas, and Cronbach's alpha.

Interrater Estimates of Reliability. Because many of the current commercially developed tests have open-ended items or give respondents latitude in constructing a response, judges must be used to evaluate the appropriateness of a given response. If the system of scoring responses is operating as one would hope, the scores assigned by different judges to a given examinee should be consistent. Interrater estimates of reliability reflect this aspect of consistency.

Reliability Estimates for Classifications of Examinees. The minimum-competency and CRT movements of the early 1970s emerged in response to the widespread use of standardized tests designed to facilitate comparisons among students. These latter tests were not particularly informative about what examinees could or could not do. CRT was designed to accomplish this end. Accordingly, based on performance on CRT, examinees are typically classified into one of two categories: those who demonstrated mastery of the content of the test and those who did not. In this instance, reliability is primarily focused on the consistency of these classifications. A popular measure of the extent to which examinees are consistently classified is the kappa index.

Standard Error of Measurement

The reliability statistics mentioned above are group-based statistics. A measure of the amount of error associated with a specific examinee is given by the standard error of measurement. This index can be interpreted as the typical amount of error associated with the scores of individuals. It is typically used to construct a range or interval for the scores of individual examinees.

Validity

The issue of validity is the most basic of all measurement concepts. Simply put, it poses the question of whether the instrument measures that which the user intends. This concept is so fundamental that it precedes the question of reliability in importance. If a test is not valid, then its reliability is of no importance to the user. On the other hand, a test cannot be valid if it reflects only random error. Reliability is a necessary, but not sufficient, condition for validity.

Validity is a question of test use. Any given test can be expected to be differentially valid, given the various uses to which it is put. A test designed to measure arithmetic achievement for third graders may do an excellent job for this group, but when given to students who speak a language different from that assumed by the developers of the test, it may provide little information about arithmetic achievement. The issue of validating a test is really a matter of gathering evidence to justify the use of a test for a given purpose with a particular population. This is perhaps one of the most critical issues for educational administrators.

There are several ways in which developers attempt to provide evidence of the validity of their measures. These include evidence related to (a) the content of the test, (b) the accuracy with which a test measures some underlying construct, and (c) the relationship of test scores to an external criterion measure.

Construct Validity. There are many psychological constructs which are of concern to educators. These include intelligence, motivation, self-concept, and anxiety. Commercially developed measures of these constructs are not as common in schools as achievement tests, yet they are important. Measures of psychological constructs are usually based on specific theories. Intelligence, for example, may be thought of as a global or multifaceted entity. Intelligence tests based on these two distinctly different theoretical perspectives can be expected to differ considerably. Evidence of construct validity, as usually reported in test manuals, includes a focus on the internal structure of the measure, studies of the relationship of the measure with others, and studies of groups with known characteristics.

Content Validity. Evidence that a test has content validity is based, as one might expect, on the items in the test. The question of content validity concerns the extent to which the items on a test reflect the type of content and cognitive skills expected by the user. Within the context of content validity, the term *instructional validity* is often used. This is a key idea that poses the question of consistency between what was taught and what is represented in a given test. To the extent that there is a mismatch, a test has limited utility for drawing inferences about student achievement.

Predictive Validity. This type of validity is usually reported for tests designed to predict some future event. Many college admissions tests, for example, report validity coefficients related to their ability to predict freshman grade point averages. Similarly, many aptitude and intelligence tests report validity coefficients, which are indexes of the extent to which the measure can predict valued outcomes such as grade point averages and class rank.

Consequential Validity. A final issue discussed in the context of validity is the notion of consequential validity. Again, building on the dependence of validity on test use, this type of validity is concerned with the consequences of test use. For example, if a student was administered an interest inventory and interpreted the results in terms of what he could or could not do, the results could be said to have a negative impact on the student's aspirations. The general idea is that the use of any measure should be evaluated in terms of its potential impact on those involved.

Test Scores and Norms

In the definition of a standardized test presented above, it was noted that not only was test administration standardized, but the interpretation of results was also standardized. This observation is based on the fact that a point of reference is needed to give a test score meaning, and a uniform point of reference is needed to ensure standardization. For example, it is true that a score of 5 has no meaning in and of itself. To give this score meaning, we could say either that it represented a perfect performance on a test or that it was higher than the score received by, say, 90% of the other examinees. This distinction is between an absolute and a relative interpretation of test performance.

Criterion, Domain, and Standards-Based Interpretations of Test Scores. A true criterion-referenced interpretation of a test score would involve comparing the score to some fixed performance standard. If passing an exam meant that a student should answer 75% of the items correctly, then the criterion would be 75%. Using this criterion, students could be classified as either "masters" or "nonmasters." During the minimum competency testing movement, most states reported mastery classifications for examinees.

A domain-referenced interpretation of a test score is focused on interpreting the scores relative to the proportion of the domain a student has mastered. If the domain of interest were simple addition, a domain-referenced interpretation of a test score would involve estimating the percentage of items in the domain the student could answer correctly. For example, if a domain was narrowly defined as all the sets of two single-digit numbers (e.g., 1 + 1 = ??), then a sample of items drawn from this domain could be used as a test and the percentage of the items a student could answer correctly on the test could be used to estimate the percentage he or she could answer correctly in the domain.

A standards-based interpretation of a test score is a type of criterion-referenced interpretation, but instead of focusing on, say, the percentage of items in a domain an examinee can answer correctly, the focus is on the level of proficiency examinees are able to demonstrate. Typically, several levels of proficiency are established and, based on examination results, examinees are classified accordingly.

Norm-Referenced Interpretations of Test Scores. Relative comparisons or interpretations of test scores are based on a direct comparison of an individual's performance with some norm group. Test users must consider the age and appropriateness of the norms before informed use can occur. Outdated norms have been the basis of severe criticisms of standardized achievement tests (see Cannell, 1988). Similarly, inappropriate norms have been used as a basis for charges of discrimination or test bias. Norms can be based on the scores of individuals or groups such as schools. Group norms should be the basis for interpreting group-level statistics (e.g., school means), and individual norms should be the basis for interpreting the performance of individuals.

Relative comparisons are usually accomplished with three broad categories of scores: percentiles, normalized scores, and expectancy scores. A percentile expresses an individual's score relative to the position of other scores in a group. The question answered with a percentile rank is the following: What percentage of the persons in the norm group had this score or lower? The higher the percentile rank of a score, the better the performance.

Normalized scores come under a variety of names: norm-curve equivalents, stanines, T scores, and so on. All share the characteristic that the raw score or number correct is transformed to a score with a given mean and standard deviation. For example, stanines have a mean of 5.0 and a standard deviation of 2.0. They facilitate comparison of an individual's performance across content areas, assuming the norm group is the same.

The final type of scores considered in this chapter is expectancy scores. Broadly speaking, these scores summarize performance relative to the expected standard. Age- and grade-equivalent scores are expectancy scores. A grade equivalent provides information about an examinee's performance compared to others in neighboring grades and provides answers to questions such as whether a student is reading at grade level.

Different Types of Standardized Tests

In the past, when educators discussed standardized testing in schools, they were almost always concerned with a group-administered examination which consisted of multiple-choice, matching, or true-false items. The chief purpose of the exam was to compare the performance of students, or some aggregate such as a grade or school, to performance trends locally and nationally. Today, what is meant by a standardized test has evolved to include portfolios of student work, examinations based on open-ended items with more than one right answer, samples of products produced by examinees, and even oral presentations and performances. Tests are designed not only to facilitate the comparison of students with others, but to identify specifically what students can and cannot do, and, more important, to foster teaching and learning of valued skills. In this book, I consider two broad categories of tests: intelligence and aptitude tests and achievement tests.

Intelligence and Aptitude Measures

Measures of intelligence or aptitude are typically focused on what examinees have the potential to do. Although there is a tendency to equate performance on these measures with innate, fixed capacities, most in the measurement community readily argue that these measures reflect learned skills which are modifiable. The types of skills measured with intelligence and aptitude tests are generally broader than those reflected in achievement tests and are usually not linked to a specific instructional experience, but instead reflect general skills useful in learning in a variety of contexts and content areas. These skills include (a) memory, (b) pattern analysis, and (c) abstract reasoning. Intelligence tests can be group-administered or individually administered. Group-administered measures are more common in schools because they are relatively inexpensive and do not require a lot of time to administer. In contrast, individually administered measures usually require a trained specialist, can be prohibitively expensive, and may take days to administer. These are usually reserved for questions concerning students with special needs.

Intelligence and aptitude tests are intended to provide additional information about the learning potential of individual students. Some are designed to yield a single overall measure of ability, whereas others yield multiple and more specific indicators. Measures which produce a single global measure of ability are usually based on a specific theory of intelligence and are useful for predicting achievement in a variety of different learning situations. However, for any given setting (e.g., content area or course) they are likely to have less predictive power than measures which yield scores for multiple abilities.

Intelligence and aptitude tests have many uses in schools. They are used to group students, identify students with special needs, select students for special programs, and aid in counseling and vocational guidance. These applications are problematic when (a) decisions are based solely on the basis of ability measures, and (b) ability measures are treated as fixed and innate rather than as learned behaviors which are affected by environment, motivation, and a host of other factors. Largely because of inappropriate uses, ability measures have been at the center of a continuing controversy in education. The relationship between performance on intelligence and aptitude measures and a student's social background, race, or gender has led to questions of bias and prompted the development of culture-fair tests (for an extended discussion, see Wigdor & Garner, 1982).

Achievement Tests

Unlike intelligence and aptitude tests, achievement tests are designed to reflect a student's performance over a defined content domain. Achievement tests may be multi-battery measures which yield scores on a variety of different content areas, single-battery measures which are focused on a specific content area, or diagnostic measures. Multi-battery achievement measures are common in state assessment programs. Some of the more popular ones include the Iowa Tests of Basic Skills, the Cognitive Test of Basic Skills, and the Stanford Achievement Tests. In addition to producing scores in a variety of content areas (e.g., reading, mathematics, social studies), most have multiple levels which facilitate following a student's academic growth from elementary school to high school graduation. Multi-battery achievement measures are ideal for drawing conclusions about a student's relative strengths and weaknesses in various content areas.

Multi-battery achievement tests sample a variety of content areas, but to make the exams manageable, each content area is sampled only sparingly. As a consequence, the more specificity that is required about a student's performance, the less satisfactory these measures are. Single-subject measures provide the type of detailed information about a student's performance in a particular subject area that can be used for instructional planning. Diagnostic measures not only provide a level of specificity not found in multi-battery measures, but they also provide information about the enabling skills required to perform certain tasks.

CONCLUSION

Standardized tests have a long and controversial history of use in schools (for a thorough review, see Walker, 2000). In recent decades, they have been criticized for their perceived negative impact on teaching and learning. Regardless of this controversy, however, they are likely to play an increasing role in education. Because of this fact, it is important that administrators be aware of the basic characteristics of standardized tests. This chapter presented a basic overview of standardized tests. Their construction, technical foundations, and uses in education were discussed. Later chapters provide more detail on issues of test preparation activities.

SOURCES OF INFORMATION AND ADDITIONAL READINGS

Standards for Evaluating Standardized Tests

American Educational Research Association, American Psychological Association, and National Council on Measurement in Education. (1999). *Standards for educational and psychological testing*. Washington, DC: APA.

This book presents guidelines formulated by a joint committee of the American Educational Research Association, American Psychological Association, and National Council on Measurement in Education. It presents explicit guidelines on test construction, fairness issues, and test application. This document serves as a guide for test developers and those that publish reviews of published tests. It is an essential reference for anyone who may need to evaluate a test.

Critiques of Tests

The *Mental Measurements Yearbook*, published by the Buros Institute, is an annual publication of critiques of some of the most popular tests used in education and psychology. The SilverPlatter service produces a CD version of the yearbook (www.silverplatter.com/catalog/mmyb.htm).

Information About
Standardized Tests

Perhaps the best source of information on tests in the information age is the Education Resource Information Center Clearing House on Assessment and Evaluation (www.ericae.net). This site provides links to most large publishers of tests (e.g., Educational Testing Service, Psychological Corporation), reviews of published tests, ratings of state testing programs, a test locator service, and even test selection tips.

National Council for Measurement in Education (www.ncme.org)

This is a primary site for measurement specialists in education. Here you will find discussions of key issues and a wealth of information on specific topics.

Educational Testing Service (www.ets.org)

This is the site for the largest testing company in the world. ETS is responsible for the Scholastic Assessment Test

(SAT) and a host of other examinations. A visit to this site is a must.

Bias and Fairness
Issues in Standardized Testing

The National Center for Fair and Open Testing focuses on the fair and equitable use of tests in education, employment, and other settings. Their Web site (www.fairtest.org) has a wealth of information for anyone with concerns about test use.

Additional Readings

Linn, R. L., & Gronlund, N. E. (2000). *Measurement and assessment in teaching.* (8th ed.). Columbus, OH: Merrill. This is a shorter work than the others, but very informative.

Rudner, L. M., Conoley, J. C., & Plake, B. S. (1989). *Understanding achievement tests: A guide for school administrators.* Washington, DC: The ERIC Clearinghouse on Tests, Measurements, and Evaluation. This is a brief and concise guide which can be a good start.

Thorndike, R. M. (1997). *Measurement and evaluation in psychology and education* (6th ed.). Columbus, OH: Merrill. This is an excellent source or follow-up to the material presented in this text. The coverage is comprehensive and user friendly.

Worthen, B. R., White, K. R., Fan, X., & Sudweeks, R. R. (1999). *Measurement and assessment in schools* (2nd ed.). New York: Longman. This is an excellent guide for the administrator, with a good outline for a school testing program.

2

Standardized Test Preparation for Schools: A Model

This chapter presents the school test preparation model, which is the focus of this book. Because the creation of an effective test preparation program is ultimately about school improvement and change, we start by focusing on the school improvement literature and what researchers suggest about making positive changes in schools. We then present the basic test preparation model. At the end of this chapter, we provide information about promising whole-school improvement designs and the national comprehensive school reform movement.

THE BANDWAGON OF SCHOOL CHANGE

Every few years, it seems, there is a new cure for the ills of public schools. The Effective Schools movement of the early

1980s, spearheaded by Ron Edmons at Harvard University, was widely embraced as a means for transforming poor-performing inner-city schools into effective learning environments. The model was widely accepted by the educational community in the United States and abroad, in many instances becoming the basis for statewide reform efforts. The Accelerated Schools and Total Quality Management movements also seemed to be solutions for addressing the needs of these same schools. To this list one could add many other programs, including Success for All, the Coalition of Essential Schools, and the Modern Red Schoolhouse (Stringfield, Ross, & Smith, 1996).

There is evidence that, of the many programs designed to improve schools, some have led to positive changes in student learning (Slavin & Fashola, 1998). However, it is also true that the majority of efforts over the past several decades have not lived up to expectations (Murphy & Adams, 1998). Whether this is because the programs were internally flawed or inappropriately implemented is open to debate. What seems clear is the decidedly bandwagon aspect to educational reform efforts in the United States (Svoboda & Wolfe, 1974). Innovations appear on the educational scene with a great deal of excitement, followed by widespread adoption, only to fail to live up to expectations and be replaced by a newer innovation. For most of the history of educational reform in this country, as some have observed (Slavin, 1989), rather than following a rational scientific progression, school reform appears to resemble changing fads in the fashion industry, a bandwagon of change riding on a wave of excitement and popularity, but lacking substance.

LESSONS LEARNED AND THE ESSENTIAL ELEMENTS OF SCHOOL CHANGE

Beginning in the late 1980s or early 1990s, U.S. educators began to move away from the populist pattern of educational change in which innovations were adopted largely on the basis of philosophical persuasions or intuitive appeal. Educators and policymakers started to ask for sound empirical evidence that an innovation was effective or that it was based on empirically supported principles and procedures. Questions about what works and what does not seemed to dominate school change debates as never before (e.g., Kohn, 1993). This trend is not only present in the professional journals, but reflected in federal initiatives and legislation such as President George W. Bush's new education bill, No Child Left Behind, and the Improving America's Schools Act (www.ed.gov/legislation/ESEA). Both explicitly require empirical evidence that school innovations work or that they are based on empirically supported principles and practices.

In addition to support from empirical research, there is growing evidence of a consensus on the basic characteristics of an effective school improvement or change program. Several large-scale literature reviews (Hoachlander, Alt, & Beltranena, 2001) as well as requirements of federal programs such as the massive Comprehensive School Reform and Development Program (see Hale, 2000) all point to several key principles of school change.

Change Must Be Systemic

One of the lessons that appears to have been learned from the past is that piecemeal, fragmented, and add-on approaches to improving schools simply do not work. For example, since its beginning in 1965, Title I of the Elementary and Secondary Education Act relied on a pull-out design in which identified students were taken out of their classes and given special assistance. However, with its reauthorization in 1994, and based on recommendations from the RAND Corporation, the federal government encouraged and supported schoolwide efforts. The basic logic, supported by empirical data, is that whole-school designs are more successful than piecemeal, fragmented approaches because they engage more components of the organization and operate in a more coherent fashion (Le-Tendre, 1996). Glennan (1998), in discussing the New American Schools designs, writes

> The NAS (New American Schools) initiative is based on the premise that high-quality schools possess a design. Such a design may be explicitly and carefully articulated, or it may exist as a set of well-developed understandings among teachers, students, and parents that have evolved through time but have never been explicitly committed to paper. A design articulates the school's vision, mission, and goals; guides the instructional program of the school; shapes the selection and socialization of staff; and establishes common expectations for performance, behavior, and accountability among students, teachers, and parents. It provides criteria for the recurring self-evaluation and adjustment that are essential to continuing improvement in any organization's performance. It makes clear the student behaviors the school expects when it accepts a student and the nature of the work environment a teacher must accept if he or she takes a job in the school. (p. 11)

Glennan goes on to note that the majority of U.S. schools lacks a coherent design. Instead, he argues, "they are homes for a collection of activities and programs of varied origins" (p. 11). This is probably an accurate description of more than half the schools currently operating in the United States. The activities Glennan refers to are likely the remnants and adaptations of a litany of central office, state, and federal mandates; pet projects of administrators and supervisors; and a varied collection of practices based on the experiences, preferences, and "connections" of individual teachers. What seems true is that in such a setting, initiatives are likely to work at cross-purposes: they may receive limited support, but they are unlikely to receive the type of commitment from stakeholders that can lead to real change. In contrast, a coherent program of change focuses on curriculum, instruction, assessment, professional development, school management and finance, parent and community support, and the needs of individual students. A whole-school approach to change, as some have noted, does not focus on any aspect of the organization in isolation, but explicitly or implicitly involves all of the systems of the organization (Hoachlander et al., 2001).

Change Must Be Guided by a Shared Vision With Measurable Goals and Benchmarks

This is perhaps obvious, but it warrants emphasis—positive change requires a direction. It requires a sense of where an organization is (status), where it wants to go (goals), and what the important milestones are along the way (benchmarks). Research on schools that work consistently reports a common sense of direction and purpose among administrators, faculty, and students (see Hoachlander et al., 2001). Of the many whole-school designs recommended by the U.S. Department of Education, all emphasize the importance of a unifying vision, concrete and realistic benchmarks, and communication on progress as key elements of school effectiveness (see Hale, 2000). A lack of measurable outcomes has been a common characteristic of many failed school reform efforts of the past.

Change Must Involve All Key Stakeholders

Change requires the active participation of those responsible for implementing it (Schmoker, 1999). The literature is replete with instances in which federal, state, and local mandates fail to significantly change the instructional experiences of students because the teachers and administrators at the building level are not committed to the initiative. A similar outcome is often associated with top-down initiatives from principals in which teachers and staff serve only a passive role. Implementation requires participation, not only to ensure that expected innovations actually occur, but to build on the strengths and resources of the local personnel. The Accelerated Schools, Coalition of Essential Schools, and Paideia models, to name a few, all emphasize the importance of having parents, administrators, teachers, and students actively involved in school improvement efforts, from conceptualization through implementation and evaluation (see Wang, Haertel, & Walberg, 1998). Similarly, the Comprehensive School Reform Development Program requires participating schools to have an active plan for parent participation and evidence of the commitment of school staff.

Change Must Be
Planned and Incremental

Key lessons from past efforts at reforming schools include initiatives often failing to move beyond the planning stage, supporters often expecting instant outcomes, and initiatives often stalling due to poor coordination of scarce resources (Streifer, 2000; Stringfield, 2000). It is true that many whole-school designs entail considerable expense. However, as reported by those engaged in the change process, with careful planning, school personnel can find ways to absorb these expenses (e.g., rearranging schedules and assignments). An effective reform program coupled with an ineffective and unrealistic implementation program is almost assured of failure. To combat this, the vast majority of current reform models explicitly describe a cycle of implementation which occurs in stages: (a) needs assessment, (b) preparations, (c) tailored implementation in stages or phases, and (d) evaluation and modifications. Implementation plans tend to address training needs, resource needs, changes in management and organizational routines, and timelines. Stressors which stall an initiative often can be traced to a failure to adequately address one of these planning issues.

Change Must Address the Needs and
Responsibilities of All Key Stakeholders

It has been noted that the best program for reform is useless if the people involved do not have the training and resources necessary to implement the needed changes. In the context of educational reform, this means that the professional development for teachers and school staff should address their roles in the innovation, that students with special needs should have those needs met, and that school administrators should receive the training needed to execute their roles in the process. The current literature emphasizes that professional development should not be the typical one-shot workshop which rarely finds application in the classroom, but rather should be continuous development coupled with continuous support or mentoring (see Hoachlander et al., 2001).

Change Should Be a Continuous, Evolving Process Guided by Empirical Data

As a reform process is implemented in a school setting, there inevitably is a need to adapt the initiative to the local setting. Changes in personnel, unexpected outcomes or problems, and the experiences of those involved in the implementation require and provide guidance for the evolution of an initiative. Each school presents a unique social system and any reform plan has to be adapted to the local realities. This process should be organized and not reactive as problems and difficulties occur. An organized process is one in which relevant data are collected on the implementation and impact of the initiative in a regular and timely way, and used to make decisions about changes and modifications. Decisions about the impact of change, modifications of change, and what happens next should be guided by data which reflect progress toward goals. Again, this process should be continuous and not the typical one-shot deal.

A MODEL FOR CHANGING STUDENT OUTCOMES ON STANDARDIZED TESTS

How can the essential elements of change identified above be adapted to the problem of changing student outcomes on standardized tests? Before this specific issue is considered, two questions need to be answered: First, why do students fail tests? Second, what has been done in the past to remedy student failures?

Why Students Fail Standardized Tests

With the volume of attention focused on standardized tests, one cannot help but be amazed at the large numbers of students that continue to do poorly. Yet, despite their best efforts, educators continue to struggle for an answer to the question, Why are our students doing poorly on the test? Most often, they look to students for the answers. The students, it is argued, lack motivation and do not wish to be successful, they cannot master the material, they do not have the reading skills necessary to perform well on the test, or they are not getting the necessary support at home. Rarely is there a concerted and thorough focus on the social and educational processes of the school and its test preparation practices. For the school's part, educators typically argue that students receive training on how to respond to the items on the test, are given practice examinations, and are encouraged to do well by school staff. However, when asked about the number of items on the test, the skills measured by the test, or efforts to monitor the growth of students on these skills, these same educators are usually silent. In fact, in most cases there are no efforts to appraise the effectiveness of a school's test preparation practices. In part, this is due to a reluctance to investigate the test out of fear of violation of security rules. But more specifically, this is because most schools lack a coherent test preparation design, one that is based on recognized principles of school improvement or change.

Ways Educators and Parents
Try to Prevent Student Failure

Every school has a system for preparing students for mandated standardized tests. This may sound like a contradiction to the previous statement, but it is not. A system can be well designed or poorly designed. With respect to test preparation, not all systems are created equal, and many are downright ineffective and should be overhauled or replaced. What are some of the current practices?

The Last-Minute Patch-Up

A favorite of the ineffective and disorganized administrator, this practice typically involves a schoolwide panic one or more weeks before the test is to be administered. This is followed by a total disruption of all instruction. Classroom teachers are required to give practice exams and sample items and to drill students on the material on the test. Teaching the test becomes the primary activity until the test has passed. Some students are encouraged to do well on the test and others may be encouraged, perhaps with suspensions, not to show up.

The Finger Pointing, Do Nothing Strategy

This strategy typically does not involve any organized activities prior to the test. Instead, there is a concerted effort to assign responsibility for dismal results when score reports are published in the local paper. Usually, students and parents are blamed. In such settings, the academic expectations of students are low and a norm of failure exists, not only among faculty and staff, but among students as well.

The Every Man for Himself Strategy

This strategy is a favorite in those settings characterized by strife and discord among faculty. The idea is to obtain better results than one's colleagues, particularly those who are not favored. Resources are not shared and may be hoarded. Administrators often become mediators in endless conflicts. Test scores are used to discredit colleagues and undermine any support they may receive from administration.

The Test Is Curriculum Strategy

This is common in settings where prolonged failure has given rise to desperation or where mandated tests, standards, and curriculum are poorly aligned, leaving building-level educators confused as to what to teach and how. Staff and administrators in such settings may be in line for sanctions from governing boards, and their response is to teach the test first and everything else later. Unlike the last-minute patch-up strategy, these settings are such that the test is the curriculum. Test preparation begins at the beginning of school and continues until the test is taken. Teachers favor content coverage over depth and limit the richness and authenticity of the curriculum to that which is perceived as relevant to the test. Subject areas and grades not tested become essentially second-class citizens with respect to resources.

Of course, more than one of these strategies may be in play at a given school at a given time, and they may change during the course of the school year. Further, there are other approaches which I will not mention. The point is that none of these approaches are systematic and organized in accordance with what is known about improving and changing schools, and all have the potential to negatively impact teaching and learning. What is needed is a systematic program which prepares students for the test as part of the larger goal of mastering the content of the school's curriculum.

The Four-Step Model for Schoolwide Test Preparation

One of the obvious questions from the discussion on school improvement is the implications for test preparation. Table 2.1 presents a summary which serves as the foundation for the model proposed below.

Using the principles discussed above and common features of the most popular school improvement models, the following four-step schoolwide standardized test preparation model was developed:

- Adopt a systemic approach to improvement and change

  - Create an environment of positive systemic change

  - Create an atmosphere of trust, innovation, ownership, and teamwork

Table 2.1   Summary of Implications for Test Preparation

Research-Based Principles of School Improvement	Implications for a School Test Preparation Program
Change must be systemic.	Test preparation should be a whole-school process. It should be coordinated across grades and teachers, and span the school year.
Change must be guided by a vision with measurable goals and benchmarks.	Specific and measurable goals must be set for implementation of the model as well as for evaluating the extent to which the program achieved targets.
Change must involve all key stakeholders.	Administrators, teachers, parents, and students must be involved in the entire program, from conceptualization to evaluation.
Change must be planned and incremental.	The process of implementing a test preparation program must not be the usual one-shot workshop, but a planned and incremental process over time.
Change must address the needs and responsibilities of all key stakeholders.	Test preparation must address roles and expectations of students, teachers, administrators, and parents, ensuring that each group can play its role.
Change should involve a planning, implementation, and evaluation cycle.	Test preparation should involve a continuous cycle of planning, implementation, and review or evaluation.

- Align the process with the desired output
  - Define the outcome
  - Determine information needs of stakeholders
  - Collect and analyze data on school test preparation practices
  - Analyze and summarize school test data
  - Identify and prioritize problem areas
- Align the process with the input to the system
  - Identify academic and nonacademic factors that impede student performance
  - Identify teacher characteristics that impede student performance
  - Identify social and environmental factors that impede student performance
- Create positive change
  - Identify the causes of the problems
  - Identify solutions to the problems
  - Develop a school improvement plan
  - Launch the plan, monitor progress, and make necessary changes

The objective of the model is to change the system (i.e., the school) that produced the undesired standardized test results. The remainder of the book is focused on explaining and illustrating this model. A chapter is devoted to each step and a case study is presented in Chapter 7.

CONCLUSION

The primary mission of any school is to educate children. Preparation for a standardized test should not interfere with this process. On the other hand, it is woefully inappropriate for a school administrator not to adequately prepare children for standardized tests which may significantly impact their futures, such as determining if they will be promoted from one grade to the next. An effective test preparation program prepares students to be successful on mandated tests as part of the larger goal of leading them to master the school's curriculum. The model summarized above and described in detail in the rest of the book provides a means of accomplishing this end.

SOURCES OF INFORMATION AND ADDITIONAL READINGS

American Federation of Teachers. (1997). *Raising student achievement: A resource guide for redesigning low-performing schools* (ATF Item No. 3780). Washington, DC: American Federation of Teachers.

Education Commission of the States. (1998). *Selecting school reform models: A reference guide for states.* Denver, CO: Author.

Educational Research Service. (1998). *Comprehensive models for school improvement: Finding the right match and making it work.* Arlington, VA: Author.

Fashola, O. S., & Slavin, R. E. (1998). Schoolwide reform models: What works? *Phi Delta Kappan, 79*(5), 370-379.

Herman, R., & Stringfield, S. (1997). *Ten promising programs for educating all children: Evidence of impact.* Arlington, VA: Educational Research Service.

Northwest Regional Educational Laboratory. (1998). *Catalog of school reform models* (1st ed.). Portland, OR: Northwest Regional Educational Laboratory. Available online at www.nwrel.org/scpd/natspec/catalog

Sirotni, K. A. (1985). School effectiveness: A bandwagon in search of a tune. *Educational Administration Quarterly, 21*(2), 135-140.

Slavin, R. E., & Fashola, O. S. (1998). *Show me the evidence! Proven and promising programs for America's schools.* Thousand Oaks, CA: Corwin.

Stedman, L. C. (1985). A new look at the effective schools literature. *Urban Education, 20*(3), 295-326.

U.S. General Accounting Office. (1989). *Effective schools programs: Their extent and characteristics.* (GAO/HRD-89-132BR)

Wang, M. C., Haertel, G. D., & Walberg, H. J. (1998a). Achieving student success: A handbook of widely implemented research-based educational reform models (pp. 174-177). Retrieved from www.reformhandbook-lss.org

Wang, M. C., Haertel, G. D., & Walberg, H. J. (1998b). *What do we know: Widely implemented school improvement programs.* Philadelphia, PA: Center for Research in Human Development and Education.

Comprehensive School Reform

• The National Clearinghouse for Comprehensive School Reform (www.goodschools.gwu.edu). This site provides a wealth of information for anyone contemplating comprehensive school reform. It provides a catalog of school reform models, step-by-step guides, a library of users, and a host of other resources and links, including the U.S. Department of Education (www.ed.gov/offices/OSE/compreform/).

• The Comprehensive School Reform Demonstration Program (www.sedl.org.csrd/awards.html). This site gives a list of schools that have implemented the various models.

• The American Federation of Teachers (www.atf.org). This site provides a wealth of information on school reform issues and experiences.

Additional Readings

Hallinger, P., & Heck, R. H. (1998). Exploring the principal's contribution to school effectiveness: 1980-1995. *School Effectiveness and School Improvement, 9*(2), 157-191. The authors review research from 1980 to 1995 and conclude that principals influence school effectiveness indirectly, via visions, mission, and goals.

Heath, D. H. (2000). Psychological bars to school improvement. *Education Week, 5*(27), 46, 68.

Hoachlander, G., Alt, M., & Beltranena, R. (2001). *Leading school improvement: What research says. A literature review.* Atlanta, GA: Southern Regional Education Board.

Stringfield, S. (2000). A synthesis and critique of four recent reviews of whole-school reform in the United States. *School Effectiveness and School Improvement, 11*(2), 259-269.

Stringfield, S., Ross, S., & Smith, L. (1996). *Bold plans for school restructuring: The new American schools designs.* Mahwah, NJ: Lawrence Erlbaum Associates.

3

Adopting a Systemic Approach to Improvement and Change

This chapter focuses on the creation of an environment for systemic change in a school. Systemic change is explained, and a number of steps for creating systemic change are described. The chapter ends with suggested guidelines for formulating a team of school-level educators responsible for leading the development of a schoolwide test improvement plan.

WHAT IS SYSTEMIC CHANGE?

What is systemic thinking? What does it mean to adopt a systemic approach to test preparation? First, it means avoiding the many failed strategies noted in Chapter 2. Blaming students is popular and common, but rarely brings about meaningful change. Blaming teachers is equally unproductive. A systemic approach means examining the totality of what happens to students prior to the test. It means viewing a school as a complex interconnected system, as one might think of a machine, which has inputs, processes, and outputs. Although it is important to emphasize that there are many outputs, one is student performance on a mandated test. If we use the analogy of a machine, admittedly an oversimplification, one can think of students, teachers, administrators, books, computers, and so on as inputs. The normal ebb and flow of activities in a school, that is, the arrival and departure of the buses, the routines which start the day, the instructional practices in play at any one point in time, and the policies which govern tardy students, disrespectful behavior, and so on, can be considered processes. The attitudes, behaviors, and worldviews of students as they leave the school are outputs.

Systemic thinking about student behavior on a standardized test implies that we examine the input and processes involved in preparing students for the test. It means that as we contemplate change, we focus our attention on the system which produced the current behavioral outcomes. A focus on a system is decidedly different from a focus on individuals or units. A focus on a system takes the spotlight away from an individual or unit, perhaps viewed in isolation, and turns it toward the ways in which that individual or unit interacts with others. For example, a teacher with chronic student discipline problems in her class is not simply a poor manager. The norms and expectations for student behavior in other classes are important, the rules governing the reporting of offenses to supervisors and administrators is important, and the relationship of the teacher with peers, supervisors, and administrators is important. Similarly, with a standardized test, poor performance results for a given grade in a given subject are not simply a question of poor instruction in that subject in that grade. Instructional materials are involved, norms and expectations for student achievement in other grades and subjects are involved, teacher support and training are involved, and schoolwide goals and expectations are involved. Systemic thinking means that we examine the complex interplay of factors operating to produce observed outcomes.

Systemic thinking is not a natural occurrence in most schools. Schools are highly compartmentalized, and oftentimes the world of a teacher goes no further than the classroom door. Phrases such as "their students," "my teaching," and countless others reflect the fact that many schools are a mesh of invisible lines of division. This stems in part from the fact that the teaching profession has always been typified by a significant degree of autonomy and in part because schools are loosely coupled organizations in which the component parts have considerable latitude in their operations and perhaps goals. Seeing interdependencies in ways that are constructive requires some effort in such an environment. With respect to test preparation, the implication of systemic thinking is that all stakeholders, whether or not the exams are given in the grades in which they teach or study, view themselves as an intricate part of the preparation process and that a sense of collective identity and responsibility permeates the school and extends to the outcomes on a mandated test. That is, the test is not simply someone else's problem, but the responsibility of all. Systemic thinking about test preparation means that all stakeholders are actively involved in test preparation.

CREATING AN ENVIRONMENT FOR POSITIVE SYSTEMIC CHANGE

What steps can an administrator take to create an environment for systemic change? Which policies, procedures, and actions will promote systemic change and which will not? There are several key components: make a beginning; focus on rules, procedures, and practices; and develop a collective sense of identity and purpose.

Make a Beginning

Change requires a sense of a beginning, something new. Positive change is usually focused on a new direction and purpose. Some ways of creating the excitement positive change can bring are discussed below. Here, we are concerned with setting the tone or stage. This seems trivial, but it is not. Real change usually takes time. Most people, particularly those involved in the process from a distance, usually expect immediate results. Changes in the physical environment are often the easiest and most visible ways to communicate a new direction and to inform participants that things are different. Some possibilities include painting the physical facilities; obtaining needed physical repairs, particularly those which are highly visible and suggest a lack of order and discipline (e.g., broken windows); and providing staff and teachers with desired resources. Obviously, this will depend upon to the creativity and resourcefulness of individual administrators. However, a carefully planned program of positive physical changes in the immediate environment can help sustain an initiative.

Focus on Rules, Procedures, and Practices

Rules, procedures, and practices—the ways we organize ourselves—impact behavior, norms, and perspectives. They can lead to chaos and confusion. They can also promote an unhealthy competition or positive cooperation. We promote competition when we allocate resources in such a way that some people win and others must lose. Alternatively, rules, procedures, and practices can promote cooperation and a sense of collective identity. Some procedural and other actions which promote a shared sense of identity are now described.

Promote a Collective Identity Among Stakeholders

Use the words "we" and "our." When advertisers want to get our attention, they have a few basic strategies, one of which is repetition. Constant exposure to something, perhaps an idea, seems to increase the likelihood that the idea will become part of our thinking. Use "we" and "our" and other terms which connote a collective identity as often as possible and whenever possible. Promote the use of these words among staff, teachers, and students. Such phrases as "our team" and "our parents" reinforce the idea of a collective identity. Use these in communications. Consider the following examples:

Example A	Example B
The boys on the junior football team gave it their best today.	Our boys gave it their best. Our junior football team . . .
I am very proud of the performance of the team.	We are proud of our team.
Sixty percent of the third graders scored below the Basic proficiency level on the state mandated test. They . . .	Sixty percent of our third graders scored below the Basic proficiency level on the state mandated tests. We . . .

Which examples, in your opinion, would promote a sense of collective identity? Hopefully you responded with those under Example B. These are only a few of the many opportunities administrators have to create a culture of engagement and collective identity using already established communication vehicles.

Use badges, bumper stickers, T-shirts, and other advertising tools to communicate a sense of collective identity in the school and in the surrounding community. It is an amazing fact that bumper stickers carried home by students recognized for accomplishments at school, not just test scores, always seem to *actually* find their way home and usually find their way to a parent's car. They communicate an attachment and sense of collective identity for the school in the surrounding environment. Contrast this with the final destination of school newsletters, announcements, solicitations, and so on, which teachers and administrators are fond of sending home via students. The majority appear to make it no further than the floor of a school bus or the bottom of a footlocker. Why the difference? The bumper stickers are personal and positive, whereas most students are likely to see school announcements as external and extraneous. The point is that students should be actively engaged in any program to promote the school, whether on the school campus or in the larger community. For example, the school band may print T-shirts and market them to other students. The proceeds will, perhaps, be used to fund an end-of-year band trip. Depending on the graphics selected and the messages printed, the shirts offer an opportunity to increase the positive visibility of the school. When students produce the shirts, they are actively engaged in the project and increase the likelihood that the effort will be successful. Of course, there are many other possibilities.

Promote Intergrade and
Interdepartmental Collaborations With
Committee Assignments and Other Responsibilities

Most classroom teachers report student discipline as the largest problem they face. Yet, many discuss discipline issues only with close friends. Collaborations and coordination of efforts rarely occur across department lines or grades. Effective ways of promoting this include subject area teams which span several grades and strategic plans which clearly link instructional objectives across grades and departments.

Promote a Collective Purpose Among Stakeholders

Communicate the school's vision, mission, and goals to all stakeholders. It is not enough to have a shared identity—the stakeholders must have a common goal or purpose. This is the traditional role of the mission or vision statement. The reality is that the vision or mission of many schools exists only on paper. This is unfortunate because, traditionally, a vision conveys a sense of "who we are and what we value." The mission communicates a purpose, and goals specify the sequence of steps, events, or benchmarks needed to achieve the purpose. A typical vision, mission, and goal sequence may look like the following:

- *A Vision.* John J. Smith Elementary is a place where students acquire those habits of mind that lead them to be life-long learners; where they learn to value themselves and their role in society; where teachers, students, parents, staff, and administrators treat one another with respect and caring; and where all work collectively to make this a world-class school for the 21st century.

- *A Mission.* Our purpose is to prepare students to meet and exceed world-class content and performance standards in essential subject areas; to value and adhere to standards of conduct which make functioning as a citizen possible; and to value moral and ethical standards that contribute to the effective functioning of society.

- *Goals.* All students will meet national standards of performance in mathematics.

To achieve a collective purpose, however, not only must there be buy-in, as discussed below, but the vision, mission, and goal must also be communicated to all stakeholders and become part of the culture of the school. In concrete terms, the vision, mission, and goals of the school should be part of every physical space where people gather. This includes classrooms, lounges, eating areas, and any other places where there is an opportunity to convey a sense of direction and purpose. They should be communicated at public ceremonies and distributed in formal communications. They should become part of the culture of the school.

Determine If School Rules and Procedures Promote Chaos or Order

If Teacher A tells students that they are allowed to visit the restroom without an escort during class, but Teacher B tells them the opposite, a student is likely to (a) be confused and (b) perceive that rules and procedures are arbitrary. If rule enforcement and reactions to rule violations appear random, students are likely to respond with a disdain for the rules. The same can be said of teachers and school staff. Rules and procedures, if they are clear, communicated to all, and consistently enforced, can promote order and predictability in an otherwise chaotic environment. Some ways of reviewing rules and procedures for their quality and impact include the following:

- When violations occur, always question if enforcement or clarity of the rule was involved.

- Develop and undertake a carefully developed plan for communicating school rules and procedures to all stakeholders (e.g., brochures, posters).

- Develop procedures to ensure that all students, teachers, and school personnel understand the school's rules and procedures and enforce them consistently.

Create an Environment of Trust, Innovation, Ownership, and Teamwork

One of the consistent themes in the quality movement is that teamwork and cooperation are positive occurrences. This section discusses several ways of promoting teamwork and cooperation.

Use Active Participation to
Promote Ownership and Cooperation

Actively participating in the design and maintenance of an undertaking tends to promote a sense of ownership and cooperation. Some strategies to accomplish this in the context of schools include the following:

- Involve stakeholders in setting goals and priorities for the school.
- Involve stakeholders in resource decisions.
- Involve stakeholders in efforts to monitor initiatives and innovations.
- Involve stakeholders in efforts to restructure the physical environment (e.g., designing hall exhibits, creating school slogans, selecting mascots).

Encourage and Reward Constructive Feedback

Nothing seems to encourage participation as much as having an individual's ideas taken seriously. Add to this the assurance that negative feedback will not be met with reprisals and active participation is likely to result. Some ways in which feedback can be promoted include the following:

- Reward ideas and input in public and private meetings by signaling value. Avoid negative characterizations of input (e.g., " That was stupid.") or the contributor (e.g., "You are stupid.").
- Recognize the most positive actions to promote the school's efforts or initiatives.
- Develop means for constant input and feedback, such as suggestion boxes placed in various locations of a facility.
- Actively solicit feedback on all aspects of the system, both formally and informally, from all stakeholders. What is working and what is not? What needs to be done differently? This can be accomplished with interviews, focus groups, and so on.

Actively Foster Teamwork and Cooperative Efforts

Teams are usually more effective than individuals. Teams can be as loosely defined as an agreement to share ideas that work, or they can be extensive joint efforts. Some suggestions for promoting teamwork and cooperation include avoiding comparisons which foster envy or competition among teachers, departments, or grades. Such comparisons may be important, but public displays can often be detrimental to a sense of "we." Also include public assistance to neighbors and teamwork in school recognition and reward systems.

Reward Initiative and Creativity

In order for a system to be effective, the creativity and experiences of all stakeholders must be involved. An environment in which all stakeholders feel that their ideas are likely to be taken seriously and experimentation is not frowned upon is one in which the creativity and ingenuity of individuals are likely to blossom. Private and public approval and recognition of initiative and creativity by stakeholders serve to increase the likelihood of their reoccurrence.

STEPS TOWARD REALIZING SYSTEMIC CHANGE FOR TEST PREPARATION

We have already discussed making physical changes in the environment and developing plans to promote a collective identity and a collective purpose in the school. But how do we move this from the administrator's personal reflections to the faculty, staff, students, and parents? There are several concrete steps which can help: awareness training, the creation and support of a school change team, and the establishment of policies which promote an environment of trust, innovation, and teamwork, that is, buy-in.

Awareness Training to Set the Stage

The School's Vision, Mission, and Goals

The first topic on the agenda for an awareness training session is the vision for the school as created by the agent of change, the administrator. As the example presented earlier illustrated, this vision should be fairly general because once the culture of "we" is established, input from stakeholders will lead to changes. A vision based on the experiences of previous efforts to change schools should not be a top-down event, but a collective event involving all stakeholders. As the agent of change, however, the first steps toward this process lie with the chief administrator. The vision, as noted above, will not only address questions such as "Who are we?" and "What do we value?" but can also address what we will look like when we arrive at our desired destination, what benefits will accrue to us, what will be said about us, and what will be different in terms of our physical environment, the resources and rewards we possess, and the attitudes and behaviors of the school family. It is almost assured that the initial vision of the future as articulated by the principal will undergo some change as the school change team begins its work and a culture of "we" emerges.

Identify Student Performance on the Test as a Top Priority

Given the many crises which face most schools, how is it possible to focus attention on student achievement on a standardized test and keep it there for an extended period of time? How does one avoid having test performance become the dominant theme of the school, surpassing the importance of the curriculum in the minds of many? A key to answering these questions involves understanding how each of the key groups of stakeholders (teachers, parents, and students) views the test. What, for example, are the costs to a student of doing poorly on the test? What are the personal costs, the social costs, and so on? Similarly, what are the benefits of good performance? Answers to these questions can be used to design initiatives which help sustain interest in doing well on the test, while not leaving the broader curriculum in the background.

Initiatives Targeted at Parents

In most settings, parents do not play an active part in test preparation for their children. Most receive some communication from their child's school concerning the importance of the test, some get to view sample items, and a few may be encouraged to work with their children in specific content areas. For the majority, however, guidance from the school regarding test preparation involves little more than the suggestion that they send their children to bed early the night before the exam is to be administered. This can be changed by preparing materials for parents which specifically describe the school's goals and objectives for the standardized test and clearly articulate what home activities will support the school's efforts. This should go beyond the typical "Make sure Johnny gets plenty of sleep the night before. . ." to specific activities which can support the teacher's instructional objectives. Other ways of communicating to parents regarding the test preparation program include the parent teacher association (PTA), school meetings, and newsletters.

What about the curriculum of a school? Do parents need to know what students are expected to learn, including, but not limited to, the test? Obviously, the answer is yes. However, in most cases, parents have only a vague idea as to what cognitive and intellectual changes they can expect in their children as a result of, say, sitting in Ms. Smith's third grade class from August to May. In most cases, they point to test scores. This is not a problem if the test score is an accurate reflection of a child's proficiency with respect to the school's curriculum. However, as noted above, any test is only a sample of the broader domain of the things adults want children to know. Further, most standardized tests tend to reflect the subset of skills which are easily measured, not necessarily those complex skills which are most valued in children by adults (e.g., the ability to execute complex projects). The implication of this is that a school should not limit its parent initiatives to just those skills likely to be included on a test, but instead should educate parents on the broader curriculum and ways in which they can be actively involved. Fortunately, the variety of resources available for parents is greater than ever before.

The following publication is from the Web site of the Louisiana Educational Assessment Program (LEAP): Helping Your Child Succeed in School (www.doe.state.la.us/DOE/pdfs/helpchildsucceed.pdf). What makes this publication particularly useful is that it clearly articulates the achievement outcomes of eighth grade students in English language arts and identifies the types of questions they are likely to encounter on the exam. The publication even suggests general

Sample Resources for Parents on the World Wide Web

How can I encourage my young child to read?	www.eric.ed.gov/resources/parent/read.html
How can I be involved in my child's education?	www.eric.ed.gov/archives/involved.html
How can I improve my child's reading?	www.eric.ed.gov/archives/reading.html
Getting online: A friendly guide for students, teachers, and parents	www.eric.ed.gov/resources/online/index.html
Summer home learning for parents and children K-3	www.ed.gov/pubs/Recipes/reck-3.html
Helping your child get ready for school	www.ed.gov/pubs/parents/GetReadyFor School/index/html
Tips to help your child in school	www.doe.state.la.us/DOE/asps/home.asp?I = PARENTS
Ready Web Virtual Library: Tips for parents	http://readyweb.crc.uiuc.edu/parents.html

guidelines for parents. This model can serve as a starting point for efforts of a school level team.

Initiatives Targeted at Teachers, Staff, and Students

To make sure teachers are constantly on target for test preparation, there are several things which can be done. One of the problems faced by many administrators is apathy toward standardized testing. Most mandated assessment programs consist of a combination of norm-referenced and standards-based assessments. Student promotion may be associated with the standards-based assessment, but not the norm-referenced results. School accountability may be differentially affected by the two tests, which are not given equal weight in all grades in a school. The result is that many stakeholders conclude that they do not have an active role to play in test preparation. For example, in a program in which fourth grade test results impact school accountability, but third grade results do not, the third grade teachers may feel that they have less at stake and a lesser role than do the fourth grade teachers. This mindset may be encouraged by the administrator through differential allocation of resources among the two grades, with Grade 4 being favored. An important principle of a systemic approach to test preparation is that preparation must begin prior to the grade in which the test is given. To accomplish this, the administrator can strive to develop a collective sense of responsibility for test preparation among all stakeholders.

Prioritizing student performance on the test can be accomplished in a variety of ways separate from the official directive to appeal for cooperation. The best strategies communicate the reason for the priority so that all stakeholders buy in. The consequences of poor performance usually work well as a means of communicating the importance of a particular activity. If a state accountability program is linked to teacher pay, student promotion, and so on, all stakeholders need to be made aware of this. Pamphlets can be distributed to teachers and parents, and even official meetings can be used to stress the importance of the test. Students can be told in exact terms that test performance can and will impact promotion to the next grade. A note of caution: It was noted above that a testing program can run away with a school's curriculum, resulting in a short-term gain, but many long-term losses. A test should not be the top priority of a school. Among top priorities, performance on a test should not be the only priority related to academic achievement. This will almost certainly produce a form of teaching to the test, which is unhealthy. Some more specific guidelines follow.

There should be continuous attention to top priorities, including student performance on the standardized test, throughout the school year.

For each of the target groups (teachers, staff, and students) address the following:

- Personal costs of poor performance

- Personal benefits of good performance

- Social costs of poor performance

- Social benefits of good performance

Specific activities for reinforcing the importance of the test:

- School bulletin boards which report on schoolwide academic activities, including test preparation activities

- School newsletters with sections dedicated to test preparation

- Public recognition for persons or groups exhibiting positive attitudes and actions related to academic accomplishments, including test preparation

- Periodic and public status reports (e.g., principal announcements, PTA meetings) on progress or activities

- Test preparation training for all stakeholders that focuses on the role each can play

- A grade or department level monitoring system for reviewing classroom activities

Familiarize All Stakeholders
With the Systemic Approach to Change

Once the parents, students, faculty, and staff of a school have become oriented to the standardized test and its importance to the mission of the school, knowing that the "blame" for any negative results is not on "us" is one of the most effective ways to solicit the cooperation of all involved. This is true of teachers, staff, and students as well. To be effective, an administrator must make sure that all groups understand that the initiative was designed to target the system, not them. This point can be emphasized through public announcements, small group meetings, and so forth.

Communicate Concrete
Goals and Objectives of the Change

If all stakeholders know where they are headed, they are much more likely to become actively involved. If they have a stake in setting the direction, they are even more likely to get actively involved. If goals and objectives are stated for the entire school, not just a particular grade, a broader sense of purpose is apt to follow. A well-articulated vision for the entire school is a means of emphasizing the collective identity so important to a systemic perspective. Some specific ways in which to communicate school goals include the following:

- School posters which list specific subject area objectives by grade
- Teacher brochures which list school level subject by grade objectives and which could also include sample test items, instructional strategies, and so on

Communicate the Long-Term
Perspective of Change and Improvement

This is done to avoid the sense of failure which comes when expectations are not met. External support systems are particularly notorious for espousing the notion that results should be immediate and once something is done, it is done forever. Reinforcing the idea that change is a long-term commitment can be done by constantly repeating the long-term perspective and setting goals and objectives for extended periods of time. In Chapter 6 we describe test-related goals set for five or even ten years into the future.

Selecting and Preparing a School Change Team

One way to ensure the failure of a plan is by not providing the necessary resources for its success. There is considerable work involved in developing a plan for changing test scores. The team charged with carrying out this task must be effective if the initiative is to be successful. Below, I list several questions, which if answered early on, can help promote the effectiveness of the team.

What Should Be the Charge and Structure of the Team?

If the team knows exactly what is expected of it, it is much more likely to accomplish that end than if it has to create purpose and direction as it goes. The model described in this text lists four broad categories of activities for the test preparation team: defining the target, aligning the target and the process, aligning the process with inputs, and monitoring progress. Each of these categories has specific activities which can be assigned to the team.

Who Should Be on the Team?

Few things are as destructive to the effectiveness of a school-based team as internal conflict. This could stem from personality differences, differences in levels of motivation, competence, and so on. The nature of interpersonal relationships on a team should be monitored and considered during the creation of the group. Basing a team on volunteers, building on preexisting relationships, and having personal knowledge of the competencies and levels of motivations of individuals are all factors which could be taken into consideration.

What Resources Should Be Made Available to the Team?

According to teachers, the scarcest resource for school committee work is the time to actually do the work. As with most school improvement models, the administrator is often faced with the choice of hiring substitutes or instituting some type of creative scheduling. The work described here is intensive, particularly early on. School resources will almost certainly have to be diverted from other activities to this one. In many settings, poor outcomes on a standardized test carry such dire consequences for the entire school that diverting resources from other activities for this enterprise is justified. This justification is enhanced if the focus of the team's work centers around the entire curriculum of the school, not just mandated standardized tests.

What Power and Authority Will the Team Have?

The administrator must be astute in setting the team's boundaries. Ambiguity regarding what is and is not appropriate for the team can lead to friction and chaos as the team interacts with other teachers and school staff. As an example, is it appropriate for the team to observe classes, or should this be left to persons responsible for teacher evaluation? Should the team have access to teacher tests and instructional plans? There is no one-size-fits-all answer for this issue. The decisions regarding what the team can and cannot do must be made by the administrator, with due consideration to the dynamics of the particular school.

How Will the Team Be Monitored?

Any and every team must be monitored. Monitoring the activities of a group is not an invasion of privacy and need not be considered micromanagement. In fact, monitoring a group promotes productivity. An ineffective team rarely gets things done in a timely manner and is often characterized by internal conflicts and poor attendance or participation. Minutes from meetings, regular reports, and informal interviews with team members not only communicate value and importance of the group, but also provide valuable information about its function.

Table 3.1   Checklist for Creating an Environment for Positive Systemic Change

---

Make a beginning
- Remove things in the physical environment which connote disorder and chaos
- Make positive changes in the physical environment (e.g., landscaping)

Focus on rules, procedures, and practices

Promote a collective identify among stakeholders
- Use the "we" word
- Use advertising tools to promote attachment and identity
- Use intergrade collaborations to promote collective identity

Promote a collective purpose among stakeholders
- Communicate the school's vision, mission, and goals to all stakeholders
- Determine if school rules and procedures promote chaos or order
- Create an environment of trust, innovation, ownership, and teamwork
- Use active participation to promote ownership and cooperation
- Encourage and reward constructive feedback
- Actively foster teamwork and cooperative efforts
- Reward initiative and creativity

What Will Happen If the Team Is Not Effective?

Unfortunately, it is true that despite the best planning and preparation possible, things can go wrong. Some school-based teams will simply be ineffective. The most common problem is that nothing gets done: team meetings are poorly attended, no concrete decisions are made when meetings occur, and even if decisions are made, there is no follow-up. In these circumstances, the team must be replaced.

CONCLUSION

This chapter describes the process of creating an environment in which constructive change is possible. It is true that schools

Table 3.2   Steps Toward Realizing Systemic Change for Test
Preparation

Step 1. To set the stage for change, conduct awareness training
sessions for all stakeholders
– Review and reinforce the school's vision, mission, and goals
– Identify student performance on the test as a key target of
the change
– Explain the importance of performance on the test
– Provide empirical data on previous, current, and
expected outcomes
– Familiarize all stakeholders with the systemic approach to
change
– Focus on the system, not individuals
– Reinforce collective identity and purpose
– Stress importance of teamwork and cooperation
– Communicate concrete goals and objectives of the change
– Communicate specific goals with respect to inputs,
process, and outcomes
– Communicate the long-term perspective of change and
improvement

Step 2. Select and prepare a school change team
– Determine the charge and structure of the team
– Determine who should be on the team
– Determine what resources will be made available to the team
– Determine what power and authority the team will have
– Determine how the team will be monitored
– Determine what will happen if the team is deemed to be
ineffective

which have poor test scores one year are likely to have poor
test scores the next year, schools with high teacher turnover
one year are likely to have high teacher turnover the next year,
and so on. The point is that while the superficial aspects of a
school may change frequently, the basic processes and outcomes are remarkably stable. Changing outcomes on a test
means changing these basic processes. If the focus is not on
changing basic processes to improve student learning, then
many of the stopgap, unethical, and even illegal practices
described in Chapter 2 are likely to characterize a school's test

preparation program. The purpose of this chapter was to describe procedures and steps by which a climate for changing basic processes can be created. These procedures and steps are summarized in Tables 3.1 and 3.2. The next chapter focuses specifically on the standardized test as a catalyst and important target for positive change.

SOURCES OF INFORMATION
AND ADDITIONAL READINGS

Brassard, M., & Ritter, D. (1994). *The memory jogger: A pocket guide of tools for continuous improvement and effective planning.* Methuen, MA: GOAL/QPC.

Deal, T. E., & Peterson, K. D. (1999). *Shaping school culture: The heart of leadership.* San Francisco: Jossey-Bass.

Downey, C. J., Frase, L. E., & Peters, J. J. (1994). *The quality education challenge.* Thousand Oaks, CA: Corwin Press.

Fields, J. C. (1993). *Total quality for schools: A suggestion for American education.* Milwaukee, WI: ASQC Quality Press.

Hopfenberg, W. S., Levin, H. M., Chase, C., Christensen, S. G., Moore, M., Soler, P., Brunner, I., Keller, B., & Rodriguez, G. (1993). *The accelerated schools resource guide.* San Francisco: Jossey-Bass.

4

Aligning the Educational Process With Desired Outcomes

I t is difficult to confront a challenge unless something is known about its nature. Unfortunately, this fact often seems lost when test preparation is the issue. In this instance, there is often an astounding lack of information among key stakeholders, including parents, students, and even teachers. Facts such as the number of items on the examination, the format of the items, and the content emphasis of the exam are often a mystery to the students who must take the test and the parents and teaches who must help prepare them. Later in this chapter, I recommend that administrators survey students, teachers, and parents to ascertain the extent of factual knowledge about the test among their consumers and employees. I suspect that many will be astounded at the results.

In this chapter I describe ways of gathering and communicating factual data about standardized tests. I also describe techniques administrators can use to determine the test preparation process their school currently uses. As noted earlier, every school has a test preparation process. These processes can range from very formal programs with written documentation to those which are extremely informal and highly unstructured. Recognizing and understanding the process is a critical step toward improving it.

Following the discussion of the test preparation process, the chapter turns its focus to the task of interpreting and analyzing score reports which test publishers and state education agencies prepare for local schools and school systems. The final section presents a discussion of ways to identify problems in the test preparation process.

Defining the Outcome

Why define the outcome? Defining the outcome has three chief advantages: It simplifies the task of setting concrete objectives, it provides structure and focus for preparation activities, and it removes anxiety and confusion associated with uncertainty.

What is meant by defining the test? Most stakeholders are likely to have basic information such as the name of the test, some sense of its level of difficulty, and, perhaps, some knowledge of the types of items and questions involved. However, are key players in possession of the information they need to be able to play a meaningful role in preparation activities? That is the real question. For example, if we want parents to be involved in test preparation, then what information should they have? Further, once this information has been gathered, how should it be communicated to parents so that they can best use it? These same questions can be asked of students and teachers. The answers to these questions are as follows: First, determine what information is needed by each stakeholder, and second, with input from each target audience, prepare a strategy for communicating the outcome.

DETERMINING INFORMATION
NEEDS OF STAKEHOLDERS

Conduct an Information Needs
Assessment for Each Target Group

Based on an understanding or projection of the roles the groups will play, determine their information needs. Also, contact representatives of each group to ascertain what information they would like to have and what roles they foresee themselves playing. For example, classroom teachers and instructional staff will need detailed information about the content emphasis of the test, the number and types of items, the objectives measured by the test, and so on. This may be represented in the form of a checklist as follows:

1. Every teacher should have a copy of the test blueprint.

2. Every teacher should have a copy of the objectives measured by the test.

3. Every teacher should have sample items.

4. Every teacher should have a summary compiled by the test preparation team.

In contrast to teachers, students may simply need to know what types of skills, in a general sense, are measured and with what types of items. A similar abbreviated summary may be all that is required for parents in terms of factual knowledge. But, this should not be left to speculation. Developing a table or chart similar to Table 4.1 is recommended.

Identify Sources of Information About the Test

There are far too many sources of information about standardized tests to justify the lack of knowledge found in many schools. Several of the more popular publications and Web sites are listed at the end of this chapter and in Chapter 1. The more useful outlets are (a) school district offices, (b) state

Table 4.1   Information Needed About the Test

Target Group	Projected Test Preparation Role	Information Needs
School administrators	Procuring resources Monitoring grade and subject area progress	Number of items and skills measured
Supervisors and department heads	Coordinating instruction and resources Evaluating progress	
Classroom teachers and instructional staff	Providing instruction regarding test content Monitoring student progress	
Students	. . .	
Parents	. . .	

departments of education, (c) libraries, and (d) the test publishers themselves—their Web sites are usually filled with insightful information about their products. The most useful documents include technical reports, administration and interpretative guides, instructional guides, and old or outdated forms of the exam.

Have the Test Preparation Team Construct Summaries for Each Target Group

The team should construct summaries which include, but are not limited to, the following: content and skill emphasis, item formats and instructions, student response procedures, reading level, and potential cultural or gender bias problems. Table 4.2 is an example of a partial summary.

Of course, the effort to acquire information about a standardized test must not violate system or state policies. Thus, it is *highly* recommended that prior approval be obtained from these

Table 4.2   Number of Items by Subject Area

Subject area	Minutes	Grade 3	Grade 4	Grade 5	Grade 6
Vocabulary	20	21	20	22	24
Reading comprehension	45	14			
Spelling	12	20			
Mathematics	35	12			
Totals	112	67			

Notes.
1. All directions for individual items must be read independently by the student.
2. Six items will contain stimulus material related to fishing, sewing, etc.
3. The reading level of the test is grade 4.
4. The instructional emphasis is as follows:
   - Objectives 1–6, five multiple-choice items
   - Objectives 7 and 8, four context-dependent items

sources before initiating the data collection process. Finally, the checklist in Table 4.3 summarizes these recommendations with regard to defining the outcome.

COLLECTING AND ANALYZING DATA ON SCHOOL TEST PREPARATION PRACTICES

The process a school uses to prepare students for a standardized test is difficult to determine and is rarely fully understood by examining written documentation. Instead, in this section I recommend a series of steps.

Construct Lists of Objectives for Each Domain on the Test

This, ideally, would have been done in the previous phase. Nevertheless, this document should present a list of the objectives measured by the test that is as extensive as concerns about test security and local policies will permit.

Table 4.3   Checklist for Defining the Outcome

1. Obtain information about test
   a. Sources: District office, state department of education, libraries, test publishers
   b. Documents: Technical reports, instructional guides, interpretive guides, old forms of exam, and so on
   c. Publications: *Buros Mental Measurements Yearbook, Tests in Print*, and so on

2. Have team of teachers summarize test at *your* school with regard to
   a. Content and skill emphasis
   b. Item formats and instructions
   c. Student response procedures
   d. Reading level for *our* students
   e. Potential cultural and gender bias

3. Have team of teachers compile documents that can be shared with all teachers at our school

Survey or Interview Teachers to Determine Which Objectives They Teach

Once classroom teachers are familiar with the domains and objectives measured by the test, the next step is to have them document which of those objectives they address in their classes and when. Also, it is useful to determine when they reinforce those objectives. Table 4.4 is an example of such a survey form.

Review Teachers' Examinations

The purpose of this step is to determine the consistency between classroom assessments and the content and cognitive skill levels of the test. This review provides valuable information about what teachers are reinforcing in their classroom assessments relative to the test. This information can be obtained by reviewing samples of classroom assessments for content and skill emphasis in Tables 4.5 and 4.6.

Table 4.4   Teacher Test Preparation Survey

Teacher Name:_____	Grade:_____		Date:_____	
Objective	Week 1	Week 2	Week 3	Week 4	Week 5
OBJ1					
OBJ2					
OBJ3					
OBJ4					
OBJ5					

Pencil in: IN, Direct instruction was (will be) provided for this objective during this week.
RI, This objective was (will be) reinforced during this week.
NA, This objective was not (will not be) addressed during this week.

Table 4.5   Review of Teacher Examinations: Consistency between Classroom Assessments and Test Objectives

Objective	Questioning	Midterm	Final	Projects
OBJ1	Yes	No	Yes	No
OBJ2				
OBJ3				
OBJ4				
OBJ5				

Observe Classes to Determine Consistency Between Instruction and Content and Skill Desired

This step is probably the closest to what is usually involved in teacher review and evaluation by administrators

Table 4.6   Review of Teacher Examinations: Cognitive Emphasis
of Sample of Objective Assessments

Objective Measured on the Test	Cognitive Emphasis of Objective	Cognitive Emphasis of Teacher Examination	Matching Status (Yes/No)
OBJ1	Knowledge	Knowledge	Yes
OBJ2	Comprehension	Knowledge	No
OBJ3	Analysis	Knowledge	No
OBJ4			
OBJ5			

and supervisors. The difference is that these observations are
timed to focus on objectives specifically included on the test.
The intent is to determine the consistency between the objective and the actual instruction. Procedures currently used for
teacher review should be used. In Chapter 3 the question was
raised as to whether this was a function which could or
should be carried out by the school test preparation or
improvement team. The answer to this will depend on the
interpersonal dynamics of the specific setting and is important to consider.

Gather Information on Instructional Coverage from Students

An often overlooked source of information about classroom instruction is the student. Students are in a good position to describe what was covered, when it was covered, and
how effective the coverage was. One way of gathering this
information is to have selected students keep journals on their
classes (see Table 4.7).

Table 4.7   Student Classroom Journals

Objective Stated in Concrete Terms	Date Covered	Effectiveness of Coverage (Did You Get It??)	Date Included on an Examination
How to divide fractions			
How to multiply fractions			

Survey or Interview Teachers to Determine Specific Test Preparation Activities

Given the high-stakes nature of standardized testing, most teachers in affected grades are involved in some type of preparation activity. Such activities may range from using items similar to those on the test to directly teaching test items. Part of the process of building a schoolwide program is to determine whether classroom teachers have used appropriate or inappropriate test preparation activities, to understand what has worked in the past, and to see if test preparation has resulted in a neglect of the broader curriculum of the school. If the tables presented above are expanded to include a school's curriculum for each grade, it is possible to determine if teachers have allowed test preparation to replace the school's curriculum. Also, knowing what has worked for

Table 4.8   Sample Map of School Test Preparation

	Week 1	Week 2	Week 3	Week 4	Week 5
OBJ1	INS T1	R1 T2	R1 T2	RE	TEST
OBJ2	NA	NA	NA	INS T1	TEST
OBJ3	INS T1	NA	NA	NA	TEST

Notes.
INS, Student receives instruction on objective.
R1, Class activities reinforce objective.
RE, Review objective for test.
T1, Liz Jones (classroom teacher)
T2, Dave Smith (classroom teacher)

teachers in the past provides a means for sharing effective and perhaps creative strategies which go largely unknown by colleagues or even supervisors and administrators.

Survey or Interview Administrators and Supervisors to Determine School-Level Activities

Every school has a plan. Knowing what the strategy has been is important to understanding what may or may not work in the future. Administrators should have this knowledge.

Compile Information Into a Map of the School's Test Preparation Process

Once the data listed above have been gathered, the next step is to compile it into a form which will reveal potential problems and strengths. Table 4.8 is an example.

What does this pattern in Table 4.8 suggest about the test preparation practices at this school? First, the students could probably be expected to do quite well on objective 1. In

Table 4.9   Checklist for Analyzing the Process

1. Construct list of objectives for each domain on the test

2. Survey or interview teachers to determine
   - Which objectives they teach
   - When they teach those objectives
   - When they reinforce those objectives

3. Review teachers' exams to determine
   - Consistency between content and skill of objectives
   - Instructional emphasis

4. Observe classes to determine
   - Consistency of instruction with objectives (types of questions, etc.)

5. Have sample of students keep journals
   - What was covered this week
   - How many students learned it

6. Survey or interview teachers to determine how they prepare students for the exam
   - When do they start
   - What do they do

7. Interview administrators, supervisors, and so on to determine
   - What school-based activities prepare students for the exam
   - How are problems identified and dealt with

8. Have team compile summary of findings and flowchart the process
   - Look for consistency across data sources and determine what actually happens

---

contrast, they could be expected, other things equal, to do quite poorly on objective 3. In fact, a map such as this could not only cover the grade in question, but also previous grades with respect to related skills.

This section has focused on analyzing the process by which a school prepares students for a standardized test. The recommendations offered in this section are summarized in the checklist in Table 4.9.

ANALYZING AND SUMMARIZING
SCHOOL TEST DATA

Having arrived at an understanding of how the school prepares students for the test, in this section we try to ascertain the
consequences or outcomes. There are three basic objectives:

1. Determine what the pattern of student performance has
   been over time.

2. Make predictions about what the trend indicates for the
   future.

3. Have all stakeholders engage in a process of identifying
   problem areas.

Characterizing Student
Performance on Standardized Tests

This section is focused on summarizing student performance on the test. These summaries are based on the types of
score reports typically produced by test publishers.
Depending on whether the test is norm-referenced or criterion-referenced, the types of information will differ.

Norm-referenced tests (NRTs) are designed to provide
information about a student's performance relative to a comparison group. As noted in Chapter 1, this comparative information is usually based on a national sample of the content
typically taught in a given subject area in a given grade.
Because NRTs are designed to be as widely applicable as possible, their relevance to any given school may be somewhat
limited. It is important, therefore, to correlate the objectives
measured on an NRT with the instruction provided to
students as part of the review process (the test mapping
process discussed above). This correlation should be examined
prior to trying to make sense of any NRT score report.

Developers of NRTs typically produce score reports for
individual students, teachers, and grades, as well as at the
building level. The scores typically reported include national

Table 4.10 Sample Norm-Referenced Test Student Score Report

Student Name: Grade:				
	National Percentile Rank (NPR)	Stanines (ST9)	Norm Curve Equivalent (NCE)	Grade Equivalent (GE)
Reading	23	3	23	3.4
Language	45	4	56	3.7
Social Studies	55	5	77	4.1
Mathematics	65	6	89	4.2

and local percentile ranks (NPRs and LPRs, respectively), standardized scores such as stanines (ST9s) and normal curve equivalents (NCEs), and growth and development scores such as grade equivalents (GEs) and age equivalents (AEs). Table 4.10 is an example of an NRT report.

The NPR score represents the student's national percentile rank for each of the subject areas. In the example, compared to students nationally, this student is weakest in reading. An important next step would be to look at the subskills in reading and try to identify the specific areas where the student is weakest. The NPRs also indicate that the student is relatively strong in mathematics. Stanines have a mean of 5.0 and a standard deviation of 2.0. Only mathematics is above the mean, and reading is clearly below. Stanines can be averaged at the teacher, grade, or building level. The NCE presents information similar to the ST9, but has a mean of 50 and a standard deviation of 21.06. It also can be averaged. The GE presents data on the individual student relative to students in given grades. In this case, assuming that this student is a fourth grader, he is below grade level on both the Language and Reading subtests. These would indicate areas where possible improvement is called for.

At the teacher, grade, or building level, these data would be averaged when possible. For example, the average ST9 might be reported by grade level as a means of determining the performance of a teacher or grade over time. Because it is an ordinal measure, the NPR should not be averaged and is usually summarized by examining quartiles, for example, the percentage above the 50th national percentile. If this value is below 50, then students in a given class, grade, or building are performing less well than students nationally.

In contrast to norm-referenced tests, criterion-referenced tests attempt to describe student performance with respect to standards. Many states use the categories associated with the National Assessment of Educational Progress (NAEP). For example, in Louisiana, the standards-based assessment program characterizes student performance into one of five proficiency levels: Advanced, Proficient, Basic, Approaching Basic, and Unacceptable. Each level of performance represents a range of possible scores on the test and can be characterized with respect to the types of competencies students have been able to demonstrate. Typically, score reports are produced at the student, teacher, grade, and building levels. Performance results are presented by subject area (e.g., reading, language arts, mathematics) and for clusters of objectives. Because of its link with school accountability, administrators focus strongly on the percentage of students at or above the Basic proficiency level.

Summarizing Student Outcomes

Standardized test results should be summarized in such a manner that trends and patterns can be linked directly to the test preparation process in a school. Summaries and trends should be produced at the building level, the department level, the grade level, and even at the level of the individual teacher. Test developers produce a variety of reports: individual reports for students and parents; class-level reports for teachers; and grade-, department-, and building-level reports for supervisors and administrators. In some cases these reports can be tailored to specific settings, but in most cases the types of information reported and how they are presented are predetermined. That this may be problematic is attested to by the fact that, in most schools, standardized test reports find little use, either because educators are uncomfortable with the information on the reports and what it means or because they question its relevance. In either event, it is likely true that the types of questions that teachers, supervisors, and other building-level personnel have about the outcomes of students on the test are not readily available in off-the-shelf score reports. For this reason, it is important for building-level educators to play an active role in summarizing test data. This process starts with a thorough review of score reports currently available from the publisher; in other words, there is no reason to reinvent the wheel. This review should include teachers, supervisors, and administrators with the focus being, What questions about student outcomes on the test are not answered by the score reports? Two of the more typical outcomes of these sessions are as follows:

- Reports (graphs and tables) are needed which reflect student performance for a given grade, teacher, and so forth over time.

- Reports are needed which directly contrast performance of subgroups of students (e.g., males–females, high ability–low ability, minorities–majority) for a given grade, teacher, and so forth over time.

Examples of each type of report are presented below for subscales typically used with standardized norm-reference tests. Table 4.11 reflects differences in student outcomes for variables considered to be important by educators. The information presented is at the teacher level, but can be aggregated to the grade, department, or even building level.

A similar strategy of summarizing outcomes can be used to reflect growth from the previous year. See Table 4.12. Again,

Table 4.11 Comparative Test Results

Teacher Name: _____ Grade: _____ Date: _____

	Ethnicity			Gender			Socioeconomic Status			Attendance			Ability		
	B	W	Di	M	F	Di	H	L	Di	H	L	Di	L	H	Di
Total Reading															
Vocabulary															
Reading Comprehension															
Total Mathematics															
Problem Solving															
Procedures															
Total Language															
Language Mechanics															
Language Expression															
Science															
Social Studies															
Total Battery															

Note. Di, Difference in percentage above the 50th national percentile.

Table 4.12   Comparative Summary of Student Test Data Over Time

Teacher: _____   Grade: _____   Test: _____   Year: _____

	All Students			Male Students			Low Socioeconomic Status			High Ability			Low Ability		
	02	03	Di	02	03	Di	02	03	Di	02	03	Di	02	03	Di
Total Reading															
Vocabulary															
Reading Comprehension															
Total Mathematics															
Math Problem-Solving															
Math Processes															
Total Language															
Language Expression															
Science															
Social Studies															
Total Battery															

Note. Di, Difference in percentage above the 50th national percentile.
02, Percentage above 50th national percentile in Grade ___ during the 2001–2002 school year.
03, Percentage above 50th national percentile in Grade ___ during the 2002–2003 school year.

Table 4.13   Summary of Instructional Objectives

Teacher: _____ Grade: _____ Students = ALL				
		Percentage in 1-3 Stanine Range		
Content Area	Objective	2001-2002	2002-2004	2004-2005
Mathematics	Division of fractions	23%	15%	35%
	Addition of fractions	15%	23%	35%
	Subtraction of fractions			
Biology	Knowledge of cell structure			

these results can be aggregated to the grade or higher level and, to some extent, control for extraneous variables with regard to a teacher's impact. They therefore help account for differences among groups of students as test results are examined over time.

In addition to reflecting general patterns for subject areas, it is also important to summarize results for clusters of instructional objectives within content areas. Table 4.13 presents summaries for low-performing students, that is, those in the bottom three stanines.

Graphs are also useful for monitoring and characterizing student outcomes over time. Depending on the nature of the testing program at a given school, it may be meaningful to follow a cohort over several years. Any of the data presented in table form above can also be presented graphically. The first graph (Figure 4.1) assumes a school testing program in which

Figure 4.1   Graph of School Outcomes Over Time

Percentage

	1996	1997	1998	1999	2000	2001	2002	2003	2004	2005
96 +										
91-95										
86-90										
81-85										
76-80										
71-75										
66-70										
61-65										
56-60										
51-55										
46-50										
41-45				G4	G4	G4	G4			
36-40			G4							
31-35		G4					G3			
26-30	G4					G3				
21-25				G3	G3					
16-20		G3	G3							
11-15	G3									
6-10										
0-5										

School Year

Note: G3, Grade 3; G4, Grade 4; G5, Grade 5; G6, Grade 6; G7, Grade 7; G8, Grade 8; G9, Grade 9; G10, Grade 10; G11, Grade 11; SCH, schoolwide.

Figure 4.2   Graph of Comparative Outcomes

Percentage

Percentage	1996	1997	1998	1999	2000	2001	2002	2003	2004	2005
46-50										
41-45										
36-40										
31-35										
26-30										
21-25										
16-20										
11-15										
6-10							D3			
1-5	D1			D1	D2	D2				
0		D1	D1							
1-5										
6-10										
11-15										
16-20										
21-25										
26-30										
31-35										
36-40										
41-45										
46-50										

School Year

Note. Shaded area represents positive values.
D1, Percentage difference between minority and majority students.
D2, Percentage difference between males and females.
D3, Percentage difference between high ability and low ability students.

a given multilevel test is administered in all grades, which allows for monitoring progress over time.

By changing the vertical axis to allow for negative values, this same graph can be used to present the comparative data summarized earlier (Figure 4.2).

The range of possibilities for summaries of test data is unlimited. For example, classroom teachers may be interested in summaries which identify students with strengths in specific content areas or with specific clusters of objectives. It is necessary for educators to note that summaries based on a limited number of cases tend to fluctuate more than those based on numerous cases.

IDENTIFYING AND PRIORITIZING PROBLEM AREAS

The tables and graphs generated above, when added to reports produced by the test publisher, should provide the data necessary to identify problem areas in the outcomes of a school test preparation program. A guiding principle of this process should be that the closer the identified problem is to the source of the instruction, the more likely an effective solution can be found. Also, by considering both trends and absolute performance levels (perhaps relative to some performance standard or goal) for different breakdowns of the data, the school test preparation or improvement team can sort test outcomes into priority categories (see Table 4.14).

Those outcomes in Category 1 in Table 4.14 reflect areas of strength. In contrast, those in Category 4 have both a negative trend and a current level of performance deemed unacceptable. Outcomes in this area are likely candidates for immediate action. However, setting priorities for a school testing program should not be solely determined by data, but should also consider other factors. In particular, two key questions are as follows: Which problems require immediate attention, and which problems, if resolved, will have the greatest impact

Table 4.14   Summary of Trend and Current Performance Data

	Current Performance Level	
Trend	Acceptable	Unacceptable
Increasing	Category 1	Category 2
Decreasing	Category 3	Category 4

or do the most good? Also, these decisions should be collective and involve all the key stakeholders in the process.

CONCLUSION

This chapter presented a variety of tools which can be used to provide school-level personnel with information about the process and outcome of test preparation. The next chapter focuses on the inputs into the test preparation process.

SOURCES OF INFORMATION
AND ADDITIONAL READINGS

Brainard, E. A. (1996). *A hands-on guide to school program evaluation.* Bloomington, IN: Phi Delta Kappa Educational Foundation.

Joyce, B., Wolf, J., & Calhoun, E. (1993). *The self-renewing school.* Alexandria, VA: Association for Supervision and Curriculum Development.

Logan, K. (1997). *Getting the schools you want: A step-by-step guide to conducting your own curriculum management audit.* Thousand Oaks, CA: Corwin.

Lyman, H. B. (1991). *Test scores and what they mean.* Englewood Cliffs, NJ: Prentice-Hall.

Sagor, R. (1996). *Local control and accountability: How to get it, keep it, and improve school performance.* Thousand Oaks, CA: Corwin.

Weinstein, D. F. (1986). *Administrator's guide to curriculum mapping.* Englewood Cliffs, NJ: Prentice-Hall.

5

Aligning the Educational Process With Inputs

A comprehensive study of a school's test preparation process should not be limited to mapping the instructional focus of teachers and diagnosing student outcomes on a standardized test. It is also necessary to ensure that the process the school uses or proposes to institute is suitable for the students who must experience it, the teachers who must deliver it, and the educational bureaucracy and community which must support it. One of the lessons learned from school improvement efforts of the past decade is that an innovation in an educational setting must be suited to the persons who must implement and use it. A carefully designed process which is not aligned with the intended audience will have little chance of success. In this chapter we focus on aligning the test preparation process with the characteristics of the students served, the teachers and staff involved, and the community context in which the school exists. In particular, we focus on obtaining data on student, teacher, and social factors which can impede the standardized test performance of students. The first section focuses on techniques of data collection and the remainder of the chapter focuses on applications related to test preparations.

TECHNIQUES OF DATA COLLECTION

Observations

Observations provide an effective means of collecting data on a variety of processes occurring in schools. Observations can be classified into three categories: observations of events, observations of performances, and observations of products. Observations of events, such as end-of-day dismissal, can provide valuable information about the social environment of a school. Groups or individuals, for example, may be observed to show a proclivity to assemble in a certain location, interact with others in a certain way, or express preferences and attitudes that they would not reveal in an interview or on a survey. Friendship patterns, communication networks, gathering spaces, and the like can all be identified with carefully constructed observations and then incorporated in a school improvement plan or process.

Observations of performances and products are typically highly structured and are designed to gather information on the maximum performance of a subject. An example of this type of observation would be an administrator observing a classroom teacher's instruction or a teacher evaluating a student project. Resources for designing and using observation techniques are listed at the end of this chapter.

Surveys

Surveys provide a convenient way of obtaining information about students and their orientation toward standardized tests, their preferences, and a variety of other issues. Surveys are a means of collecting data from a large group of subjects (e.g., an entire grade or the entire school) at minimal costs and in a short period of time. It is possible, for example, to develop surveys to determine students' knowledge and attitudes toward a standardized test and administer the survey to all students in a school. A key drawback of this approach is that the survey questionnaire assumes that its creators know the right questions to ask. Often, however, they do not. For example, the survey creators may know that students are doing poorly on an exam because they are not studying. A survey item focused on "number of hours of study" can help identify this. However, to discover that the reason students are not studying is because studying is perceived negatively in the student culture may require the developers of the survey to study the research literature, talk with experts, or conduct interviews or focus groups with groups of students. Surveys are useful, but to ensure their value, it is helpful to precede their development and administration with data collection techniques that permit more in-depth exploration of an issue. These include brainstorming, interviews, and focus groups. Themes and ideas generated with these methods can then be used to construct surveys. Resources for conducting and evaluating surveys are listed at the end of this chapter.

Interviews

Surveys can provide useful data concerning students, but they cannot provide the depth of information an interview can offer. An interview can permit the examinee to volunteer relevant information that a survey might have missed. For example, if teachers perceive that student motivation is a problem, extended discussions with students can confirm whether this is the case and can also provide insights into solutions.

There are several characteristics of successful interviews. First, the interviewer should provide the respondent with a clear understanding of the purpose of the interview, that is, why it is being conducted and how the results will be used. Second, examinees are more likely to provide accurate information about sensitive issues if they have an assurance that their responses will be kept in confidence. Third, interviewers should avoid leading activities that lead their interviewee to one type of response. These activities include asking leading or insulting questions and indicating approval or disapproval of a response. Resources for conducting interviews are also presented at the end of this chapter.

Focus Groups

Focus groups are interviews, but in this case they are with groups of students. Focus groups permit participants to build on one another's ideas and insights. They provide an easy means of identifying common themes in a group. They are limited to the extent that some individuals may be hesitant to share ideas in a public forum.

Grade-Level Exams

Grade-level exams can be a powerful way for administrators and teachers to gain intermediate information on the success of their instructional efforts. Exams designed by the instructional staff for a particular grade, which focus on the school's curriculum, can not only reinforce and ensure that the curriculum is understood, but can also provide a means for regular monitoring of student progress. Further, surveys or interviews with students, when combined with data from carefully constructed grade-level exams, can provide insights into classroom processes and their outcomes. For example, students can be asked to identify the reason they failed to respond correctly to a test item. The list of options could range from "not knowing the correct response" to "experienced a mental block." Surveys can also be developed to measure motivation for the test, buy-in to the school's goals, knowledge of the test, perceived pressure for performance, and even perceived negative peer pressure related to test performance.

Sources of surveys related to test preparation are listed at the end of this chapter. The additional readings listed in Chapter 1 provide detailed information for anyone interested in constructing surveys.

FACTORS WHICH IMPEDE STANDARDIZED TEST PERFORMANCE

There are a variety of reasons students may do poorly on an examination. These include mastery of the content represented on the test, motivation and other attitudinal factors, anxiety, self-confidence, test-taking skills, health-related issues, reading comprehension, listening skills, and study skills. Because these characteristics, and many others, can have a potent impact on student performance, it is important to gather information on any that seem relevant. In this section we offer specific recommendations for addressing these.

Health

The mental and physical health of an examinee is a factor which is often discussed in test preparation literature. Most school test preparation programs include some effort to address the physical preparation of examinees.

Some strategies for collecting information on health-related preparation include (a) interviews focused on physical preparation activities, (b) content reviews of school records and documents, and (c) anecdotal records from teachers. For example, the following items could be used to ascertain the physical test preparation practices or knowledge of examinees:

- Do you try to get six or more hours of sleep before the test?

- Did you know that being hungry during an exam will improve performance?

Anxiety

Anxiety can be an enabling factor which serves to motivate persons to perform well, or it can be disabling and lead to a type of paralysis which impedes performance. Tests are highly charged events which have the potential to motivate, but can also be debilitating for some students. Surveys, interviews, and focus groups can all be used to ascertain the extent to which students are negatively impacted by test-related anxiety. They can also be used to determine the extent to which students know about ways to manage anxiety. For example, the following survey items address test-related anxiety and responses:

- When taking tests I often can't concentrate.

- Tests make me so nervous that I often get physically sick.

- I know how to use breathing exercises to calm myself down when I get nervous.

Test-Taking Skills

A controversial topic among measurement professionals is whether examinees should be taught strategies they can use to perform well on standardized tests. The concept of *test score pollution* reflects the concern that the information tests were designed to provide can be misleading if the performance of examinees reflects their savvy with respect to the types of items presented on a given examination. Surveys can be used to determine the extent to which teachers address these skills and the extent to which students have mastered them.

Motivation

A common problem classroom teachers note is that students appear to lack motivation. Motivation for a task is a powerful factor impacting performance. Motivation reflects value, interests, and drive. If there is no buy-in to the academic agenda of a school, it is unlikely that students will demonstrate effort or commitment to performance. Surveys and interviews are powerful ways of ascertaining the level of motivation among a group of students.

TEACHERS AND STAFF CHARACTERISTICS WHICH IMPEDE STUDENTS' STANDARDIZED TEST PERFORMANCE

Teachers' attitudes, expectations, beliefs, instructional techniques, content mastery, and so on all impact the performance of students on a standardized test. A well-designed program for improving learning in school has little chance of success if teachers fundamentally believe that students are not capable of learning. Similarly, highly motivated teachers with limited content mastery are unlikely to be able to provide their students with the types of instructional experiences which will lead to positive outcomes on standardized tests. It is important, therefore, for administrators to collect and analyze data on teacher-related factors which impact test results. These include (a) test preparation practices, (b) expectations of students, (c) teachers' instructional capabilities, and (d) teachers' preferences. As with the student-level factors, these data can be addressed in focus groups, in interviews, or with surveys.

SOCIAL AND ENVIRONMENTAL FACTORS WHICH IMPEDE STUDENTS' STANDARDIZED TEST PERFORMANCE

This section focuses on the norms and social expectations students experience from their families, peers, teachers, and so on. The specific focus of this section is on norms which may impede student performance on the examination. Because

Table 5.1   Align Process With Inputs

1. Identify extraneous factors which impede student performance on standardized tests
   A. Conduct surveys, interviews, focus groups, etc.
   B. Gather data on health, test anxiety, test-taking skills, motivation, self-confidence, etc.

2. Identify academic factors that impede performance on standardized tests
   A. Conduct simulations, diagnostic tests, interviews, etc.
   B. Examine content mastery, reading comprehension, study skills, etc.

3. Identify social factors that impede performance on standardized tests
   A. conduct interviews, surveys, etc.
   B. Focus on norms and expectations from friends & peers, family, teachers, etc.

Table 5.2   Plan for Student Success on the Iowa Test of Basic Skills (ITBS)

How do we motivate students to perform well on the ITBS? Answer the following three questions:

1. What is the ITBS?
   - Brochure to parents, students, etc.
   - Simulated tests

2. How do I do well on the ITBS?
   - Teacher emphasis during instruction
   - Simulated tests
   - Test-taking skills

3. Why should I do well on the ITBS?
   - Rewards from parents
   - Rewards from teachers and school personnel
   - Rewards from friends and peers
   - Personal rewards

peers become increasingly important as students progress through school, understanding the values and orientation of peers toward the test is important. This information can also be obtained with surveys, interviews, and focus groups. The following are examples of the types of items which address the social context of test preparation:

- Do your parents want you to do well on the test? (Yes, No, Don't Know, They Don't Care)

- Do your friends want you to do well on the test? (Yes, No, Don't Know, They Don't Care)

- If you try to do well on the exam, how will your friends respond? (They Will Pick at Me, They Will Think It Is Good, They Don't Care)

CONCLUSION

This chapter focused on characteristics of students, teachers, and the social environment of the school which may act to negatively impact student outcomes on standardized tests. The focus of the chapter was on techniques which could be used to gather information about the extent to which problems may stem from any of these sources. The recommendations offered in this chapter are summarized in Table 5.1.

Table 5.2 presents the outlines of a sample plan to address student motivation for an exam. The plan was developed using information from surveys and interviews with students, parents, and teachers.

SOURCES OF INFORMATION AND ADDITIONAL READINGS

Divine, J. H., & Kylen, D. W. (1982). *How to beat test anxiety & score higher on the SAT*. Woodbury, NY: Barron's Educational Series.

Gall, M. D., Borg, W. R., & Gall, J. P. (1996). *Educational research: An introduction* (6th ed.). White Plains, NY: Longman.

Millman, J., & Pauk, W. (1969). *How to take tests*. New York: McGraw-Hill.

Orr, F. (1986). *Test-taking power*. New York: Prentice-Hall.

Taylor, K., & Walton, S. (1998). *Children at the center: A workshop approach to standardized test preparation, K-8*. Portsmouth, NH: Heinemann.

6

Creating
Positive
Change

The previous chapters have described a process of gathering and organizing data from a variety of sources. The focus was on identifying the problems which seem to negatively impact student outcomes on a standardized test. Once agreement on the problems is reached, the next steps are to identify causes of and potential solutions to the problem, implement the possible solutions, and monitor progress, making changes as needed. These steps are the focus of this chapter. We start with a discussion of ways in which educators may identify the root causes and potential solutions for agreed upon problems. These, as we note below, may come from a variety of sources. We then turn to the process of developing and implementing a plan for addressing the problems. A key component of this process is the design of a system which will permit stakeholders to monitor progress toward goals and objectives and make the necessary adjustments.

IDENTIFY THE CAUSES OF THE PROBLEMS

The previous chapters drew a distinction between the need to align a school's test preparation process and practices with desired outcomes on the test and the need to align the process with the school's input, meaning the students, parents, teachers, staff, and administrators who comprise the stakeholders. In searching for causes for the identified problems, we draw the same distinction. We first consider causes linked to the alignment of the process with the desired outcomes and then focus on the link with inputs.

Test Preparation Process

Once the actual process a school uses to prepare students for a standardized test is mapped, it can be examined for potential problems. In fact, the agreed upon problems should point, in a direct way, to some aspect of a test preparation process. For example, if the process suggests that students are performing poorly on objectives related to reading comprehension, then the aspect of the test preparation program related to reading comprehension warrants close inspection. It may be the case that the objectives are not being addressed or that they are being addressed, but not effectively. In other words, the test preparation process is a logical place to start the search for causes of a problem. There are several ways this can be accomplished.

Use Test Results as a Guide to Problem Areas in the Process

This can be done by using the problem areas identified in the test summaries described above to identify particular subject areas, clusters of objectives, teachers, subgroups of students, and so on where negative outcomes appear to be concentrated.

Compare Weaknesses Identified With
Test Data to the Test Preparation Process

In particular, consider the following:

1. Are there objectives which are not being addressed and on which students do poorly? The extent to which this may be a problem can be ascertained by comparing data on the instructional emphasis of teachers with students' performance levels and trends. For example, if surveys of teachers indicate that an objective has not been addressed or addressed only sparingly, and test data point to the objective as being an area of especially poor performance (in comparison with other areas), then the instructional focus of teachers is suggested as a potential cause of poor student outcomes.

2. Are there objectives which are being addressed but not at the appropriate cognitive level? Observations of classroom instruction, reviews of examinations and assignments, and so on can all be used to characterize the cognitive level of instruction provided to students. Data from these sources can be compared to the cognitive levels of the test as described in documents provided by the test publisher. Differences between the cognitive focus of instruction and that of the exam can point to possible causes of poor student outcomes.

3. Are there problems with the timing and reinforcement of particular objectives? If the test mapping process indicates a significant time lag between the time when students are being testing on a given content and the time when the content is taught, then sequencing and reinforcement schedules are possible sources of poor student outcomes.

4. Are students simply not mastering the objectives and subsequently doing poorly on the test? Grade-level examinations focused on the school's curriculum, developed by classroom teachers, and linked to the content of the standardized test of interest provide a window into the competencies of the students that is external to classroom teachers. When carefully constructed, these data can provide indications of the actual competencies of students as well as suggest sources of problems.

Input

With empirical data as a backdrop, a next resource for identifying potential causes for a test-related problem is the stakeholders. Of course, there are also external experts, central office support staff, or even theories found in the educational research literature. I believe these have a role, particularly when it comes to solutions. However, schools are in many ways like miniature societies. The Effective Schools literature describes school improvement efforts as being contextual, meaning that each setting offers a unique history, set of inter-relationships, and associations. Understanding the cause of a problem or outcome requires the participation and insights of the people involved. Toward that end, we focus on inter-actions with key building-level stakeholders, students, teachers, administrators, and supervisors, for the purpose of identifying causes of the problem.

Students

In previous chapters, students were identified as being useful sources of information about the quality of classroom instruction (Chapter 4); norms, attitudes, and other extrane-ous factors which impede achievement (Chapter 5); and even the extent to which the material on the exam was being mas-tered (grade-level tests, Chapter 5). Here, we focus on collect-ing and organizing this information to identify common and prominent themes. For example, in the grade-level test survey described in Chapter 5, if 90% of the students completing a grade-level test survey indicated that they ran out of time when taking the test, then test-taking skills are a potential cause of the negative outcomes. Student-level data can be organized into three broad groups.

1. What problems are students identifying, and do these problems relate to the problematic outcomes?

2. What problems are students having with trial tests, and do these match the problematic outcomes?

3. How do students evaluate classroom instruction, and do these results match the problematic outcomes?

In addition to the empirical data, it is also useful to engage students, perhaps in a focus group, with the agreed upon test-related problems and brainstorm the causes of the problem. Students tend to have considerable insights about the norms and processes among their peers. To the extent that key causes of the problem lie with this group, focus groups may provide useful insights.

Teachers, Staff, Administrators, and Supervisors

Teachers, staff, administrators, and supervisors are essential stakeholders to involve in the identification of potential causes of problems. They often have unique insights into the inner workings of a school and are frequently in the best position to identify systemic problems. Although there are many possibilities and techniques for guiding interactions with these groups, brainstorming sessions and one-on-one interviews seem to work as well as most.

The final step in the process of identifying the cause of the problem is for the school test preparation and improvement team to compile information from the various sources and identify the primary causes of the identified problems. Primary causes are simply those things which are identified with the greatest frequency. These should be shared with the key stakeholders.

IDENTIFY SOLUTIONS TO THE PROBLEMS

Identifying solutions to the problems brings this process back to the school improvement movement. It is important to consider insights from key stakeholders (students, teachers, staff, administrators, and supervisors), but outside solutions should also be entertained. The process for acquiring input from students and other building-level stakeholders can be similar to the process used above for acquiring insights into the causes of the problem. In fact, the same brainstorming sessions which are used to identify the causes of the problems can, and should, be used to identify potential solutions. However, so that this process benefits from the experiences of school improvement efforts, the process of evaluating potential solutions, to the extent possible, should be driven by supporting data and evaluation.

External solutions to educational problems abound in the literature. In earlier chapters we discussed various online and other resources for identifying improvement programs to address school-related problems. Again, however, the posture has to be one of careful adaptation followed by evaluation.

DEVELOP A SCHOOL IMPROVEMENT PLAN

Once the problem, its causes, and prospective solutions have all been identified, the next step is to develop a plan for implementing the solution. To accomplish this, there are four key questions which should be answered. In this section, we discuss each in turn.

What Are Our Objectives?

Concrete objectives are an essential component of a test preparation plan. A vague statement such as "We want our students to do well on the test" provides little guidance for either taking specific actions or evaluating outcomes or progress. Objectives for test performance should state specific, but realistic, outcomes and should indicate the amount of time involved. As an example, the following objective provides a clear target for fourth grade teachers, supervisors, students, and parents:

By the year 2010, 95% of the students enrolled in Grade 4 will achieve the Basic level of proficiency on the Language Arts subtest of the state-mandated criterion-referenced test.

Table 6.1   Growth Targets

School Year	2004-2005	2005-2006	2006-2007	2007-2008	2008-2009	2009-2010
Growth Target	55% (Base Year)	63%	71%	79%	87%	95%

Note. This growth target was computed as follows: (Objective - Base Year)/Years in Cycle. The expected growth per year is 8 percentage points.

This objective is measurable and provides a means for setting benchmarks which can be used to evaluate progress toward this outcome. For example, if this objective were established during the 2004–2005 school year, specific growth targets could be set for each year from fall of 2006 to fall of 2010. If in fall 2005, the base year, the percentage of fourth grade students scoring at the Basic proficiency level was 55%, interpolation would yield the growth targets presented in Table 6.1 for the years 2006 to 2010.

Benchmarks translate long-range plans and goals, which may seem formidable, into concrete smaller changes. They provide a way for gauging progress on a regular basis.

Who Will Do What?

Many school improvement efforts are stalled because of a belief that only external experts can solve the problems. In fact, the required expertise often exists in a school system or is readily available from state education agencies. As part of implementing an intervention, the following should be considered:

- What can be done in-house?
- What assistance can be obtained with little or no expense?
- What assistance can be obtained from outside experts?

How Will the Intervention Be Monitored?

A system for monitoring the outcomes and the implementation of an intervention is essential. It is critical to know what has been done and to be able to gauge, on a regular basis,

Table 6.2   Activity Summary Report

Activity Summary

Objective: _____

_____

Activity	Target Audience	Number of Participants	Date	Evaluation/ Follow-Up

whether the activities have had the desired effect (see Table 6.2). In terms of monitoring what has been done, we noted earlier that regular reports from the school test preparation team can provide this information.

Reporting the status of the overall plan, however, may require some reports not available from the test publisher. Some examples are provided in Table 6.3. Table 6.4 presents a summary of status as being met, not met, or partially met.

What Is the Timeline?

Developing a realistic plan for implementation of the intervention and communicating it to stakeholders facilitates monitoring and helps combat unrealistic expectations. The timeline should specify a start date, implementation milestones, and the review cycle.

The steps outlined in this section are presented in the checklist in Table 6.5.

CONCLUSION

This chapter focused on the identification of causes of problems, the identification of prospective solutions, and the

Table 6.3   Progress Report

Progress Report

Teacher: _____   Grade: _____

Schoolwide Objective: By the year 2008, 60% of our students will be above the 55th national percentile on each of the content areas of the ITBS.

Percentage of Students Above the 55th National Percentile, ITBS

	1999	2000	2001	2002	2003	2004	2005	2006	2007	2008
Vocabulary										
Reading Comprehension										
Spelling										
Capitalization										
Punctuation										
Usage and Expression										
Math Construction										
Math Problem Solving										
Math Comprehension										
Social Studies										
Science										
Maps and Diagrams										
Reference										
Reading Total										
Language Total										
Math Total										
Source of Information										
Core Total										

Table 6.4   Table for Monitoring Growth

Growth Targets for Stanford 9

Teacher: Ms. Susan Smith

Grade 5

Schoolwide Objective: By the year 2005, 60% of our students will
be above the 40th national percentile on
each of the content areas of the Stanford 9.

	Total Reading			Vocabulary			Reading Comprehension			Mathematics		
	T	P	S	T	P	S	T	P	S	T	P	S
1996												
1997												
1998												
1999												
2000												
2001												
2002												
2003												
2004												
2005												
Percentage Met												

Note. T, Target; P, Performance; S, Status; M, Met Benchmark; N,
Failed to Meet Benchmark.

Table 6.5　Checklist for Plan to Address Problems

Checklist for Developing Plan to Address Problems

1. What can be done in-house?
   - Who has the training?
   - What materials would be needed?
   - What are the budget implications?
   - Would a substitute be needed?
   - When could it be done?
   - Where would it be done?

2. What assistance can be obtained with little or no expense?
   - What is available from the district (persons, materials, funds, etc.)?
   - What is available from the state (persons, materials, funds, etc.)?
   - What is available from other sources (persons, materials, funds, etc.)?

3. What assistance can be obtained from outside experts?
   - How can outside experts be found (associations, periodicals, LDE, district office, etc.)?
   - How can outside experts be evaluated (resumes, word of mouth, etc.)?

4. What is the timeline for the intervention?
   - When will it start?
   - When will it end?

5. How will we monitor the intervention?
   a. Have a team of teachers collect and report formative data
      - Did the intervention occur (sign-in sheets, agendas, etc.)?
      - Evaluations by participants in activities
      - Evidence that changes have been implemented in classrooms (test data, student journals, observations, etc.)
   b. Set benchmarks in terms of outcomes
      - How much improvement can be expected in the short term?

development of improvement plans, including provisions for monitoring progress and making adjustments. The online and other resources cited throughout this text, including those listed at the end of this chapter, present a variety of techniques for accomplishing each of these tasks, which should assist the reader in addressing this step in the process.

SOURCES OF INFORMATION
AND ADDITIONAL READINGS

Deal, T. E., & Peterson, K. D. (1999). *Shaping school culture.* San Francisco: Jossey-Bass.

Fitzpatrick, K. A., & Edwards, B. (1998). *Program evaluation: Library media services.* Schaumburg, IL: National Study of School Evaluation.

Herman, J. L. & Winters, L. (1992). *Tracking your school's success.* Thousand Oaks, CA: Corwin.

Howard, E., Howell, B., & Brainard, E. (1987). *Handbook for conducting school climate improvement projects.* Bloomington, IN: Phi Delta Kappa Educational Foundation.

Latta, R. F., & Downey, C. J. (1994). *Tools for achieving TQE.* Thousand Oaks, CA: Corwin.

Leithwood, K., Aitken, R., Jantzi, D. (2000). *Making schools smarter: A system for monitoring school and district progress, Second edition.* Thousand Oaks, CA: Corwin.

Scheetz, M., & Benson, T. (1994). *Structuring schools for success.* Thousand Oaks, CA: Corwin.

7

A Case Study of an Elementary School

Leslie F. Jones-Hamilton, Ph.D.

This chapter describes a case study of an elementary school (K–6) in which the model was used. Although the name and location of the school are fictitious, the data reflect realistic patterns. The purpose of this chapter is to give the reader a step-by-step example of a concrete adaptation of the model developed in this text. The school I describe in this chapter is

Leslie Jones-Hamilton, Ph.D., is an assistant professor in the College of Education at Nicholls State University. Dr. Jones teaches leadership courses and serves as chair of the leadership and portfolio committees. In addition to serving as a teacher, department chair, assistant principal, and principal, Dr. Jones has also served as an external evaluator for a local school district.

not one of those in which I have worked. It is, however, a composite of many schools and educators with whom I have been involved over my educational career as a teacher, mathematics department chair, graduate student, assistant principal, principal, assistant professor, and educational consultant.

The Setting

Washington Elementary School is a K–6 grade configuration rural school with approximately 600 children, located in a fairly remote section of a midsize district as classified by the state's ranking system. There are 15 schools in the system, but the tax base fluctuates, which limits the ability of the district's supervisory staff to make long-term financial obligations. Most of the money received through state and federal funding is earmarked for operational expenses. Periodically, district employees receive bonuses. The schools in the district are fortunate to receive financial assistance from local businesses. Additionally, the majority of the students in our system are from families slightly above or below the federal definition for poverty. Approximately one third are from single-parent households with an additional 10% living with grandparents. The state ranks our district in the top 10% of districts with at-risk student populations. Within the past two years, we experienced an influx of Hispanic students enrolling in our school. The racial composition is 45% African American, 30% European white, and 25% Hispanic.

There are 30 teachers and 20 paraprofessionals on staff and their racial composition is 65% European white and 35% African American. Having experienced a turnover related to retirement about two years ago, the majority of the staff is relatively young with about a 20% veteran staff. The majority of the staff members reside in the district, which is also true of the principal and assistant principal. Both are district natives and both are young females.

Washington Elementary School: 3rd and 6th Grade Scores

	Language arts		Mathematics	
	Percentile rank	Stanine	Percentile rank	Stanine
3rd Grade	19	3	20	3
6th Grade	18	3	18	3

Scene One: The Crisis

The score reports for the state-mandated norm-referenced tests were released on May 1. As expected, we did poorly. However, no one, I think, expected things to be as bad as they were. The scores for my school indicated that 90% of the third graders and 87% of the sixth graders scored in the bottom 20%, nationally. The more damaging comparison was that there were no other schools in the system, or even in the neighboring districts, close to our dismal results.

The table above indicates percentile ranks for the third and sixth graders in language arts and mathematics. Percentile ranks range from 1 to 99 and show the student's relative position or rank in a group of students who took the tests at the same time in the same grade. The national stanine is also reported, which ranges from 1 to 9 with 5 being average.

WASHINGTON ELEMENTARY SCHOOL

Seventy-seven third graders scored at 19 in language arts; this means that 81% of students in third grade around the nation scored better than our third graders. We were not close to average. As a matter of fact, we were very close to the second stanine in both language arts and mathematics. Our sixth graders also performed poorly. The sixth grade language arts percentile rank was 18—lower than third grade.

May 1 was a Monday. By that Friday, staff morale had deteriorated to such an extent that we had a record number of teacher and student absences. The headline of the local paper on Tuesday was, "Where is the Worst School in the State? HERE." Literally, the headline was close to being accurate. The state had adopted a new accountability system that assigned school scores on the basis of standardized tests and attendance. Our school's score was among the five worst school scores in the state.

This brought the worst kind of community involvement. Parents, politicians, community leaders, and district supervisors called and came by on a daily basis. Some wanted to help, but most wanted to express outrage, and all wanted to know what would be done. Fortunately for us, the school year ended the following week, giving my staff and me the summer to devise a response. The superintendent punctuated this and gave it a sense of urgency with an unexpected end-of-year presentation to the entire staff of the school. Because I felt we had a tremendous amount of work ahead, I took the initiative to administer surveys to the faculty and students, the results of which accounted for the perceptions regarding what was emphasized as being important at school, as well as several other climate issues.

Scene Two: The Response

The district response was to send a wave of district assistance persons to help us identify and address the problems. As each came and went, it became obvious to me that there was a need for coordination. Each district person seemed to focus on one isolated issue, ignoring the broader context. The experiences and insights of my staff were overtly dismissed. Also, my staff and I were concerned that many of the things recommended could not be sustained or seemed to have little chance of working at Washington Elementary. In light of the negative publicity we received, the superintendent and the central office staff pledged to provide all of the necessary financial assistance.

Adopting a Systemic Perspective

The chaos the district support teams brought to the school during the last weeks of May far outweighed any benefits. With a great deal of effort, I managed to bring control of our response back to the building level. In early June, my assistant principal, two central office supervisors, and I started a series of extended conversations about our next steps. This group became the de facto executive council. We shared ideas and thoughts in an open manner. A norm of consensus, cooperation, and support governed our interactions and decisions. The crisis, it seems, had generated a sense of shared destiny and commitment.

One of the first decisions made by the executive group was to adopt a systemic approach to change. We viewed the problem as having many possible causes and involving all the stakeholders in the school. Immediately after the news headlines, there was a great deal of finger pointing and self-recrimination among faculty. There was a concerted effort to assign responsibility to others—including parents—and faculty with the better scores assumed little responsibility for the crisis. There was also some evidence that the negative headlines had impacted the way other students saw the third and sixth graders. Our first task was to change this among faculty and students, to create an environment for positive systemic change. Since the school year had ended, we had the summer to develop a plan. Some of the key components of the plan were as follows:

1. We would change the physical environment. We started with an extensive renewal plan for the exterior and interior of the buildings. This involved the yard, the playground, and painting the exterior walls. We also made a list of essential repairs. We felt that getting faculty and students involved in revitalizing the physical facility would help to create an atmosphere of ownership.

2. We would make a noticeable change in every space where people congregated. These ranged from new blackboards

in some classrooms to a new trophy display case in the main entrance. Motivational banners were going to be hung throughout the hallways of the school.

3. We reviewed all communications and attempted to convey the idea of a collective identity as often as possible. For example, we plugged the "we" word in every document and communication we could. The student and faculty handbooks were good starting points to plug in the word "we." We also revisited our mission statement.

4. We developed grade-level collaboration and across-grade teams of teachers, which would act to coordinate efforts. We also strengthened partnerships with the community and invited community leaders and parents to be a part of our improvement efforts.

5. We developed an assembly program for the first week of school in the fall. This program would communicate the collective identity and purpose which framed our new approach.

6. Funding was not much of a problem in that the negative publicity had made it popular for business and community organizations to contribute to our efforts. Central office also contributed. We were also determined to be proactive with respect to communicating our activities to the local media.

Defining the Outcome

We realized that we knew little about the standardized tests that had impacted our school in such a negative way. We contacted the district test coordinator and worked with this person to gather information and prepare materials from the exam. We devised pamphlets for teachers, parents, and students. The teacher summaries were detailed and listed objectives and the instructional emphasis. We decided to make these available to all teachers, not just the third and sixth grade teachers. The summaries we prepared for parents and students were identical. These addressed (a) the purpose of the exam, (b) the types of skills students needed to perform well, (d) a few sample items, and (c) the types of things which could be done at home to help prepare students for better performance. We also added a number of electronic and other resources for parents and students. It should be noted that several students and parents helped design this pamphlet.

The following is a sample of the kinds of information we included:

Student:				
Test *Vocabulary*	*Low*	*Score* *Average*	*High*	*NPR* *No. Items/* *No. Items* *Correct*
Content Area **Reading** Factual meaning Inferential meaning Evaluative meaning				
Expression Capitalization/ punctuation Usage				
Mathematics Concept estimation Numeration/ operation Geometry Measurement Fractions/ decimals/percents Probability/ statistics Equations Inequalities				

Analyzing the Process

Our next step was to determine why we had performed so poorly. At this point we brought in the members of the school improvement team. However, the dynamics of the group changed dramatically. Whether for reasons of turf or personality conflicts, the larger group failed to accomplish tasks with the same ease as the smaller group. As principal, I made the necessary adjustments. The goal was to have a team in place that could take over this work on a permanent basis. One of the realizations of the executive group early on was that this would be a long-term process, one that would require nearly full-time effort. In composing the team, I gave consideration to grade levels that teachers were teaching, areas of expertise, leadership skills, personalities, and the ability of a teacher to work on and with a team. Because this was going to be a tedious, ongoing process, I also gave great consideration to the exhibited endurance and determination levels of the staff.

After making the appropriate adjustments in the composition of the team, we set about the task of determining how we had been preparing students for the test. We assembled lesson plans that the second, third, fourth, fifth, and sixth grade teachers had submitted during the course of the year. We developed a table that indicated which objectives were addressed by which teacher and at what point during the year. The results of this exercise indicated that there was an obvious lack of coordination between the third and fourth grade teachers in the area of language arts. For instance, third grade teachers addressed sentence structure very early in the academic year, and there was no evidence that fourth grade teachers addressed sentence structure. Therefore, we could not have expectations with respect to this skill until we stressed the need for it to be addressed. Similarly, many of the mathematics objectives on the exam were not addressed in any of the grades examined. We examined the score reports and found that the third grade language arts scores were the lowest of all the content areas tested for this grade. For sixth grade, surprisingly, both math and science were poor relative to other content areas.

After we assembled the lesson plans, we also looked specifically at the tests that teachers submitted with the lesson plans. Most of the testing items across grade levels and content areas were short answer and matching. We felt that the structure of the classroom tests was not aligned with the standardized test. Teachers needed to include multiple-choice items on their tests—we realized that this had to be paced gradually.

Although there were other obvious content coordination needs, the group developed curriculum documents in language arts and mathematics sequencing instructional objectives for teachers in the second, third, fourth, fifth, and sixth grades. The curriculum documents provided coordination and continuity in the curriculum in the areas deemed most critical; and if teachers followed the sequence, it would ensure that the objectives were covered. We also developed a 36-week schedule and suggested that teachers increase weekly the number of multiple-choice items on tests.

Coordination of the curriculum and test structure alignment seemed to be obvious problems. However, the committee felt that other problems were involved. We had several brainstorming sessions, poring through the different score reports provided by the test publisher. We eventually developed a series of charts and graphs which captured the performance of students over several years and the trend, particularly for certain groups (minority students, students with poor performance in the grades preceding the grades in which the test was administered, etc.). These results indicated that although our test scores had fluctuated over the past eight years, the past four years had seen a dramatic shift downward. The following chart is a sample of one which we developed; it reports percentile ranks for minority students in our school in the area of language arts.

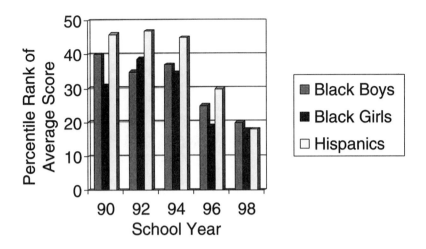

LANGUAGE ARTS PERCENTILE RANKS: TRENDS

Black boys and girls scored relatively well in 1992—with black boys close to the 40th percentile. A similar analogy is true in 1994; however, in 1996 and 1998, a sharp decline is noted. In 1998, black boys were below the 20th percentile. The same is true of our Hispanic students. Performing in 1994 near the 50th percentile and in 1996 near the 30th percentile, Washington's Hispanic students took a very sharp decline. One factor that should be noted with respect to the Hispanic population is that we experienced growth in the population at the time of the significant decline in scores.

Further, we noticed that the students who had performed relatively well as third graders (most of their grades were A's and B's) had experienced a slight increase in the percentage above the 50th national percentile on the various subtests. In contrast, those who had performed relatively poorly as third graders (most of their grades were D's and F's) had experienced a dramatic drop in the percentage above the 50th national percentile on most of the subtests.

Given these results, we asked several of the third and fourth grade teachers to join us for several brainstorming sessions. Given that it was early July, we were able to meet with about half. Nevertheless, the information they provided was very insightful. Apparently, there was a belief among several of the teachers that the best way to get test results up was to focus their energies on the better students. Personally, I thought we should focus on all students. With the implementation of the new school accountability program in the state two years before, many had started to follow this strategy.

Having teachers join the team proved to be extremely valuable. We also decided that having the insights of students might be helpful. This group also provided insights into the motivations, norms, and beliefs of their peers. As previously mentioned, I had taken initiative with administering surveys regarding climate; I wanted to have some idea of teacher and student perceptions. As teachers participated, I gained some direction on how to improve some of the negative perceptions of teachers and students. Expressing appreciation was the critical ingredient to improving positivism among the teachers, and finding ways to include students in the total environment was critical to students. Some of the things previously decided upon would assist with both student and teacher perceptions.

By the latter part of July we had made several major decisions. In addition to the curriculum sequencing in language arts and mathematics and test alignment, we decided to develop a schoolwide assessment system that would monitor progress on the entire curriculum as students moved from Grades K through 6. This process would allow us to identify strengths and weaknesses of each content area at each grade level as assessed by the performance needs of the students. We would use external resources to the extent possible, but we wanted all instructional staff to be involved in the effort. There was some pressure from the central office to limit the assessment to those objectives measured on classroom and standardized tests. However, we did not want the narrow focus of the test to drive the curriculum. Instead, we wanted to integrate the test into the curriculum in a seamless fashion.

We also decided that we would not limit the items on the test just to those types that were on the exam. Again, the reasoning behind this was we wanted to promote achievement on a variety of modalities, not just the one on a particular exam.

We also decided to consult central office (the director of instruction specifically) to develop systems for gathering information about the quality of instruction and best instructional practices related to effective teaching. The final stage was to design a plan for implementing and monitoring this effort. A key feature of this part of the process was to allow for a critical review of all initiatives associated with this program.

Scene Three: Implementation

The initial score reporting had gained negative media attention, and as a result, faculty morale and student morale had been impacted negatively. During the summer, we worked to rebuild and to focus our efforts on redirecting the crisis. The school improvement team, many other faculty members, central office staff, and school building-level administration worked diligently—our obvious goal was to improve student achievement.

Approximately mid-summer, we decided to focus on the improvement of achievement in language arts and mathematics. We realized that other content areas were important; however, our lower scores needed attention first.

The activities that we decided to implement to achieve our goal are as follows:

- Curriculum sequencing in language arts and mathematics (the team developed curriculum documents)

- Test structure and preparation (the team developed a 36-week schedule, increasing the number of multiple-choice items on the test as the weeks progressed; a test preparation period and computer lab time were added to the schedule; the goal of the test questions schedule was to gain test alignment—both classroom and standardized)

- Teacher and student motivational techniques (the administration would increase teacher observations, high-lighting a teacher of the week; students would be motivated to do homework through a reward-incentive system)

By the start of the first day for teachers, August 12, the school grounds were landscaped and a new school sign was visible. The sign and the landscaping were donated by local businesses; the older students and some faculty participated to the extent possible in restructuring the physical facility. Again, we felt like it would help students and faculty feel a sense of ownership. The central office maintenance staff completed all of the repairs and painted the interior and exterior of the building as the school improvement team and the administration brainstormed in the summer. The faculty was excited about returning to a revitalized physical structure. The entrance of the school featured a new mission statement, and positive banners were posted throughout the school.

I opted to have a motivational speaker on the morning of the first day, and in the afternoon, the school improvement team and I began laying the groundwork for the necessity of having the staff work together as a team. We presented the language arts and mathematics sequencing documents, which were received positively by the staff. In an effort to drive teacher initiative, I announced that all teachers would have planning periods daily that would allow for grade-level planning. We were able to get an additional computer lab and a librarian, which freed up time so that the administration could make provisions for the teachers' planning periods.

The additional computer lab would be a great asset because we sequenced the computer-based tutorial program to align with skills on the standardized tests. We also received a waiver from the state department of education that would allow us to incorporate a test preparation period of 30 minutes daily into our second, third, fourth, fifth, and sixth grade schedules. During the test preparation periods, teachers taught test-taking strategies and administered practice tests. Teachers would also address specific skill areas where students were deficient.

I felt it was a good time to interject in our training meeting that I would require teachers to incorporate multiple-choice items on their weekly tests and I passed out the schedule that the school improvement team developed in the summer. Several teachers were resistant to this idea; however, after I explained the reasoning with respect to classroom tests alignment and standardized test alignment, they agreed that they would try incorporating the items.

Although teachers had a daily planning period, I realized that I was expecting a lot from the teachers. I thus offered an additional incentive by starting a teacher-of-the-week program. I would make an effort to acknowledge the efforts of a teacher weekly—this teacher would receive a gift certificate from a local business, and the teacher's name would be posted on the new school sign. I felt this was also a good strategy to demonstrate appreciation of teachers.

As the instructional leader, I committed to observing teachers daily—I would alternate grade levels until I had observed all of them informally for a few minutes. I also committed to attend grade-level meetings that were to be held weekly during the grade-level planning period. Teachers realized that central office staff would perform more of the formal observations because of our test results. The supervisory staff observing from central office along with the administration would focus on identifying and reinforcing effective teaching. The director of instruction reviewed the components of effective teaching as outlined by the state department of education: management of instructional time, management of instructional behavior, and instructional presentation and facilitation. These three areas would be critical for all formal and informal observations of teachers. Throughout the school year, the director of instruction reviewed best practices and conducted workshops on critical instructional issues.

We also developed a student motivational program. Collectively, the teachers felt that homework completion was very low. We decided to hold weekly lottery drawings of prizes for students who completed all assignments during the week. The teachers felt so strongly about this that they committed to supplying the prizes. The student incentive-motivation program was successful during the year because teachers became very good in-class motivators, not just with respect to homework; we also gained parental support in this endeavor. We also pledged as a staff to include parents in as many activities as possible. We began creating monthly calendars and bimonthly newsletters that helped us to highlight faculty and students. We also kept the media informed of all the student and faculty efforts.

As the year began, the faculty was motivated and morale improved; there was also evidence of student improvement through participation in the homework drawing. I made efforts to keep the staff motivated through the faculty gift certificates, but I also wrote a lot of positive notes during my informal visits—I became very complimentary to staff. In return, they began to express appreciation for having their efforts noticed.

Among the roles I assumed was that of the schoolwide assessment system. At the end of every grading period, I observed grades and collected data from our computer tutorial program. I was able to monitor subject matter by specific skills from the computer-based program. I also analyzed results from pretests that we administered periodically during our test preparation period. These analyses helped me to realize any inconsistencies as well as areas where skill improvement was essential. I also decided to continue to administer climate surveys annually because that information had proven useful.

Scene Four: Some Results

The results of our first year showed a slight increase in performance, enough to keep the critics at bay, but not enough to get the school from under the cloud the test results had generated. We were no longer at the bottom—there were at least 15 schools below us; our school score had increased by 5 points. The language arts scores improved the most, with a slight improvement in mathematics scores. The teachers felt that the content sequencing in language arts and mathematics, the effort in teacher planning, the skills-based computer tutorial program, and the suggestions made regarding effective teaching from teacher observations were all critical for the growth in the initial year.

Personally, I felt that our curriculum had been coordinated and continuity existed—students were also getting a lot of reinforcement through the computer lab and test preparation periods. I also witnessed a change in the teachers, who were more conscientious toward students—the positivism in the environment that I attempted to model had filtered to the teachers in the classroom. It is critical that the surveys that I decided to administer prompted the need for a shift in administrative practices—demonstrating appreciation to staff. There is a strong humanistic component of educational administration which is critical to a school's climate and that many educational administrators fail to exhibit.

The school improvement team and administration worked again the following summer, and we decided to keep in place most of the activities we were using. Language arts and mathematics were identified as top priority—we felt that if we shifted, we would lose some of what we had gained and our focus should not be too broad. We made a variety of adjustments and in the second year, we were rated as "average." The threat of takeover was gone, but the success of our efforts threatened to bring our program to an end. This, in fact, was one of the greatest challenges I faced as an administrator. I constantly promoted higher goals. After three years, the school seems well on its way to becoming the best performing elementary school in the district, if not the state.

8

Conclusion

Standardized tests have the potential to improve schools. Standardized tests associated with a high-stakes accountability program also have the potential to do a great deal of damage to the teaching and learning process. Because of the objectivity standardized tests offer, it is likely that their role in accountability programs will increase in the future. As the stakes of these programs increase, pressures to improve test scores are also likely to increase. Improving test scores, in many respects, is not the major challenge for educators—there are many ways to accomplish this goal. The challenge for educators is to improve test scores and not sacrifice the quality of teaching and learning at a school. In this book, I have described a general model designed to help educators achieve this end. The model presents a series of steps which, taken together and adapted to a given setting, provide a framework for administrators to study the test, assess the extent to which the test impacts (or dominates) classroom instruction, identify problematic outcomes, devise and implement solution strategies, and monitor progress. It is hoped that administrators will take the ideas described here and launch a critical and objective review of the test preparation practices currently operating at their schools. Perhaps no one will incorporate all of the suggestions offered; however, I believe the ideas presented in this text will point many to areas where improvements can occur.

References

Bandesh, H. (1962). *The tyranny of testing.* New York: Crowell-Collier.

Brooks, T. E., & Pakes, S. J. (1993). Policy, national testing, and the Psychological Corporation. *Measurement and Evaluation in Counseling and Development, 26*(1), 54-58.

Cannell, J. J. (1988). Nationally normed elementary achievement testing in America's public schools: How all 50 states are above the national average. *Educational Measurement: Issues and Practice, 7*(2), 5-9.

Cronbach, L. J. (1975). Five decades of public controversy over mental testing. *American Psychologist, 30,* 1-14.

Falk, B. (2000). *The heart of the matter: Using standards and assessment to learn.* Portsmouth, NH: Heinemann.

Glennan, T. K. (1998). *New American schools after six years.* Santa Monica, CA: RAND.

Gould, S. J. (1981). *The mismeasure of man.* New York: Norton.

Haladyna, T. M. (2002). *Essentials of standardized achievement testing.* Boston: Allyn & Bacon.

Hale, S. H. (2000). *Comprehensive school reform: Research-based strategies to achieve high standards. A guidebook on school-wide improvement.* San Francisco, CA: WestEd.

Haney, W. (1984). Testing reasoning and reasoning about testing. *Review of Educational Research, 54*(4), 597-654.

Hoachlander, G., Alt, M., & Beltranena, R. (2001). *Leading school improvement: What research says.* Atlanta: Southern Regional Education Board.

Kohn, A. (1993). Turning learning into a business: Concerns about total quality. *Educational Leadership, 51*(1), 58-61.

Le-Tendre, M. J. (1996). Title I schoolwide programs: Improving schools for all children. *Journal of Education for Students Placed at Risk, 1*(2), 109-111.

Mehrens, W. A., & Lehmann, I. J. (1991). *Measurement and evaluation in education and psychology* (4th ed.). Chicago: Holt, Rinehart & Winston.

Murphy, J., & Adams, J. E. Jr. (1998). Reforming America's schools, 1980-2000. *Journal of Educational Administration, 36*(5), 426-444.

National Commission on Excellence in Education (1983). *A nation at risk: The imperative for educational reform.* Washington, DC: U.S. Government Printing Office. (Stock #065-000-00177-2)

Popham, W. J. (2000). *Modern educational measurement: Practical guidelines for educational leaders* (3rd ed.). Needham, MA: Allyn & Bacon.

Schmoker, M. (1999). *Results: The key to continuous school improvement* (2nd ed.). Alexandria, VA: Association for Supervision and Curriculum Development.

Shepard, L. (1991). Psychometrician's beliefs about learning. *Educational Researcher, 20,* 2-9.

Slavin, R. E. (1989). PET and the pendulum: Fadism in education and how to stop it. *Phi Delta Kappan, 70*(10), 752-759.

Slavin, R. E., & Fashola, O. S. (1998). *Show me the evidence! Proven and promising programs for America's schools.* Thousand Oaks, CA: Corwin.

Streifer, P. A. (2000). School improvement: Finding the time. *NASSP Bulletin, 84*(612), 66-71.

Stringfield, S. (2000). A synthesis and critique of four recent review of whole-school reform in the United States. *School Effectiveness and School Improvement, 11*(2), 259-269.

Stringfield, S., Ross, S., & Smith, L. (1996). *Bold plans for school restructuring: The new American schools designs.* Mahwah, NJ: Lawrence Erlbaum.

Svoboda, W. S., & Wolfe, M. P. (1974). Looking before leaping: A basic model for planning educational change. *Educational Technology, 14*(4), 62-63.

Walker, S. F. (Ed.). (2000). High-stakes testing: Too much? Too soon? *State Education Leader, 18*(1).

Wang, M. C., Haertel, G. D., & Walberg, H. J. (1998). *What do we know: Widely implemented school improvement programs.* Philadelphia: Center for Research in Human Development and Education.

Wigdor, A. K., & Garner, W. R. (Ed.). (1982). *Ability testing: Uses, consequences, and controversies.* East Lansing, MI: National Center for Research on Teacher Learning. (ERIC Document Reporduction Service No. ED213770)

Wiggins, G. (1989). Teaching to the authentic test. *Educational Leadership, 76,* 41-47.

Index

**CORWIN
PRESS**

The Corwin Press logo—a raven striding across an open book—represents the happy union of courage and learning. We are a professional-level publisher of books and journals for K-12 educators, and we are committed to creating and providing resources that embody these qualities. Corwin's motto is "Success for All Learners."